Deming Jarves

Reminiscences of Glass-Making

REMINISCENCES OF GLASS-MAKING.

BY

DEMING JARVES.

SECOND EDITION, ENLARGED.

NEW YORK:
PUBLISHED BY HURD AND HOUGHTON,
401 BROADWAY, COR. WALKER STREET.
1865.

PREFACE.

The articles upon the history and progress of Glass Manufacture herein presented to the public were originally published in the columns of a village newspaper.

They are the result of investigation upon these topics made in the few leisure moments gained from the engrossing cares of business, and consequently make no pretension to anything of literary character or execution.

The object of the writer has been to gather, in a condensed form, whatever of interesting information could be gained from authentic sources, in regard to a branch of manufacture which has attained a position among the useful and elegant arts scarcely rivalled by any other of those which mark and distinguish the progressive character of our country.

It is believed that they present, in a condensed and convenient form, much valuable information, useful alike for reference and instruction. Aside from historical or mechanical facts, there is much of romantic interest attaching to the progress of this department of art. The partiality of friends interested in the topics herein presented, rather than his own opinion of their value, has induced the writer to present the articles in a more permanent form.

BOSTON, *March* 17, 1854.

THE above was the Preface to a small pamphlet in 8vo. of the "Reminiscences of Glass-making," printed for private circulation in 1854, and now enlarged into a more permanent form, and brought down to the present year, in order to meet the demand for information which has unexpectedly sprung up from those interested in the manufacture of Glass in America.

BOSTON, *January*, 1865.

REMINISCENCES OF GLASS-MAKING.

It may be safely asserted that no department of art has, from its earliest period, attracted so much attention and investigation, none involved so extensive a range of inquiry, or been productive of more ingenious, interesting, and beautiful results, than the manufacture of glass.

The question of the origin of glass goes back to the remotest antiquity, and is involved in almost entire obscurity. All that modern writers on the subject are enabled to do, is to glean hints and indistinct statements in reference to the subject, from the very brief and unsatisfactory accounts of the ancients. These, however, throw but a feeble light upon the precise point of the origin of the manufacture; and little is proved beyond the fact of its great antiquity.

That the subject held a very prominent place in the technological literature of the ancients is clearly proved; Pliny, Theophrastus, Strabo,

Petronius Arbiter, Berzelias, Neri, Merrit, Runket, and others, referring constantly to it. The writings of all these demonstrate the deep interest existing upon the subject at their various times, but still fail to present us with any connected or detailed account of the rise and progress of the art.

When it is considered that the elements involved in the manufacture of glass are derived from the earth, — not one of its components being in itself transparent, but earthy, opaque, and apparently incapable of being transmuted into a transparent and brilliant substance,— when it is considered that from these a material is produced almost rivalling the diamond in lustre and refractive power, and sometimes so closely resembling the richest gems as to detract from the value of the costliest; can it be wonderful that in the earliest ages the art was invested with a mysterious interest attaching to no other mechanical department?

From the earliest periods, up to the eighteenth century, the art, from the peculiar knowledge and skill involved, could only minister to the wants or pleasures of the luxurious rich. The rarity of the material rendered the articles greatly valuable, as tasteful ornaments of dress or furniture;

indeed, it is well known that the glass of Venice, at one period, was as highly valued as is the plate of the present day; and the passion for possessing specimens, promised in England, at least, to excite a spirit of speculation fully rivalling that exhibited in the tulip mania, so ridiculous, as well as ruinous, in Holland.

It has been reserved for the present age, however, to render the art of glass-making tributary to the comfort of man, — to the improvement of science, — and by its moderate cost to enable the poorest and humblest to introduce the light and warmth of the sun within, while excluding the storms and chilly blasts; to decorate his table with the useful, and minister to his taste, at a cost barely more than that of one of his ordinary days' labor. That which once was prized and displayed as the treasure and inheritance of the wealthy, and which, with sacred carefulness, was handed down as of precious value, may now be found in the humblest dwellings, and is procured at a charge which makes the account of the former costliness of glass to partake almost of the character of the fabulous and visionary.

That the art of glass manufacture is destined to greater progress and higher triumphs cannot for a moment be doubted; and the time will arrive when, from increased purity of materials and progressive chemical development, the present position of the art will fall comparatively into the shade. It is no undue stretch of the imagination to conceive that lenses shall be perfected whose purity will enable the astronomer to penetrate the remotest region of space; new worlds may perhaps be revealed, realizing all that the "moon hoax" promised —

> "The spacious firmament on high,
> With all the blue ethereal sky
> And spangled heavens" —

be read as a book, and man perhaps recognize man in other worlds than his own. It may be that in its triumphs it is destined to concentrate the rays of the sunlight, and make the eye to pierce into the secrets and deep places of the sea,

> "Full many a fathom deep."

Man may be enabled to read the wonders and the hidden works of the Almighty; it may be, that the power of the traditional lens of Archimedes upon the fleet of Marcellus shall be realized, in the absorbing and igniting, and perhaps useful power of some feature of its progress; and in its sphere, the art become fruitful in practical results, rivalling the highest attainments in the department of scientific progress. It is no visionary speculation to believe, that, by the aid of machinery, it may be readily rolled into sheets, as is iron or lead now in use. It will minister more and more to the necessities and comfort of mankind, and contribute largely to the many and various manufacturing purposes of the age. That its practical adaptations are not already known or exhausted, cannot be doubted; and its applicability, in some cheaper form, for vessels of large size and certain shape, and (strange as it may seem) for tesselated and ordinary flooring and pavements, are among the results which we think yet to be demonstrated in its progress.

An elegant writer, in a late number of "Harper's Magazine," says:—

"The importance of glass, and the infinite variety of objects to which it is applicable, cannot be exaggerated; indeed, it would be extremely difficult to enumerate its properties, or estimate adequately its value. This, then, transparent substance, so light and fragile, is one of the most essential ministers of science and philosophy, and enters so minutely into the concerns of life that it has become indispensable to the daily routine of our business, our wants, and our pleasures. It admits the sun and excludes the wind, answering the double purpose of transmitting light and preserving warmth; it carries the eye of the astronomer to the remotest regions of space; through the lenses of the microscope it developes new worlds of vitality, which, without its help, must have been but imperfectly known; it renews the sight of the old, and assists the curiosity of the young; it empowers the mariner to descry distant ships, and trace far off shores; the watchman on the cliff to detect the operations of hostile fleets and midnight contrabandists, and the lounger in the opera to make the tour of the circles from his stall; it preserves the light of the beacon from the rush of the tempest, and softens the flame of the lamp upon our tables; it supplies the revel with those charming vessels in whose bright depths we enjoy the color as well as the flavor of our wine; it protects the dial whose movements it reveals; it enables the student to penetrate the wonders of nature, and the beauty to survey the marvels of her person; it reflects, magnifies, and diminishes; as a medium of light and observation its uses are without limit, and as an article of mere embellishment, there is no form into which it may not be moulded, or no object of luxury to which it may not be adapted."

In contrast with the foregoing, we will make

one more extract, from an English writer of ancient date. Holinshed, in his "Chronicles," published during the reign of Elizabeth, says:—

"It is a world to see in these our days, wherein gold and silver aboundeth, that our gentility, as loathing these metals, (because of the plenty,) do now generally choose rather the Venice Glasses, both for our wine and beer, than any of these metals, or stone, wherein before time we have been accustomed to drink; but such is the nature of man generally, that it most coveteth things difficult to be attained; and such is the estimation of this stuff, that many become rich only with their new trade into Murana, (a town near to Venice,) from whence the very best are daily to be had, and such as for beauty do well near match the Crystal or the ancient Murrhina Vase, whereof now no man has knowledge. And as this is seen in the gentility, so in the wealthy commonality the like desire of glasses is not neglected, whereby the gain gotten by their purchase is much more increased, to the benefit of the merchant. The poorest endeavor to have glasses also if they may; but as the Venetian is somewhat too dear for them, they content themselves with such as are made at home of fern and burnt stone; but in fine, all go one way, that is to the shades, at last."

PROPERTIES OF GLASS.

Glass has properties peculiarly its own; one of which is that it is of no greater bulk when hot, or in the melted state, than when cold. Some writers state that it is (contrary to the analogy of all other metals) of greater bulk when cold than when hot.

It is transparent in itself; but the materials of which it is composed are opaque. It is not malleable, but in ductility ranks next to gold. Its flexibility, also, is so great that when hot it can be drawn out, like elastic thread, miles in length, in a moment, and to a minuteness equal to that of the silk-worm. Brittle, also, to a proverb, it is so elastic that it can be blown to a gauze-like thinness, so as easily to float upon the air. Its elasticity is also shown by the fact that a globe, hermetically sealed, if dropped upon a polished anvil, will recoil two thirds the distance of its fall, and remain entire until the second or third rebound. (The force with which solid balls strike each other may be estimated at ten, and the reaction, by reason of the elastic property, at nine.) Vessels, called bursting-glasses, are made of sufficient strength to be drawn about a floor; a bullet may be dropped into one without fracture of the glass ; even the stroke of a mallet sufficiently heavy to drive a nail has failed to break such glasses. In a word, ordinary blows fail to produce an impression upon articles of this kind. If, however, a piece of flint, cornelian, diamond, or other hard stone, fall into one of these glasses, or be shaken therein a few moments, the vessel will fly into a myriad of pieces.

Glass of the class called Prince Rupert Drops exhibits another striking **property**. Let the small point be broken, and the whole flies with a shock into powder. Writers have endeavored to solve the philosophy of this phenomenon ; some by attributing it to percussion putting in motion some subtle fluid with which the essential substance of glass is permeated, and thus the attraction of cohesion being overcome. Some denominate the fluid electricity, and assert that it exists in glass in great quantities, and is capable of breaking glass when well annealed. These writers do not appear to have formed any conclusion satisfactory to themselves, and fail to afford any well-defined solution to the mystery.

Another phenomenon in connection with glass tubes is recorded in the " Philosophical Transactions," No. 476 : —

" Place a tube, say two feet long, before a fire, in a horizontal position, having the position properly supported, say by putting in a cork at each end supported by pins for an axis ; the rod will acquire a rotary motion round the axis, and also a progressive motion towards the fire, even if the supporters are declined from the fire. When the progressive motion of the tube towards the fire is stopped by any obstacle, the rotation is still continued. When the tubes are placed in nearly an upright position, leaning to the right hand, the motion will be from east to west; but if they lean to the left hand, their motion will be from west to east; and the nearer they are placed to an upright position the less will be their motion either way. If the tubes be placed on a sheet of glass, instead of moving towards the fire they will move from it, and about the axis in a contrary direction from what they did before ; nay, they will recede from the fire, and move a little upwards when the plane inclines towards the fire."

Glass is used for pendulums, as not being subject to affections from heat or cold. It is, as is well known, a non-conductor. No metallic condenser possesses an equal power with one of glass. In summer, when moisture fails to collect on a metallic surface, open glass will gather it on the exterior; the slightest breath of air evidently affecting the glass with moisture. Dew will affect the surface of glass while apparently uninfluential upon other surfaces.

The properties of so-called "musical glasses" are strikingly singular. Glass bowls, partly filled with water, in various quantity, will, as is well known, emit musical sounds, varying with the thickness of their edges or lips. When rubbed, too, with a wet finger, gently, the water in the glass is plainly seen to tremble and vibrate.

Bells manufactured of glass have been found the clearest and most sonorous; the vibration of sound extending to a greater degree than in metallic bells.

Glass resists the action of all acids except the "fluoric." It loses nothing in weight by use or age. It is more capable than all other substances of receiving the highest degree of polish. If melted seven times over and properly cooled in the furnace, it will receive a polish rivalling almost the diamond in brilliancy. It is capable of receiving the richest colors procured from gold or other metallic coloring, and will retain its original brilliancy of hue for ages. Medals, too, embedded in glass, can be made to retain forever their original purity and appearance.

Another singular property of glass is shown in the fact, that when the furnace, as the workmen term it, is settled, the metal is perfectly plain and clear; but if by accident the metal becomes too cool to work, and the furnace heat required to be raised, the glass, which had before remained in the open pots perfectly calm and plain, immediately becomes agitated or boiling. The glass rises in a mass of spongy matter and bubbles, and is rendered worthless. A change is however immediately effected by throwing a tumbler of water upon the metal, when the agitation immediately ceases, and the glass assumes its original quiet and clearness.

All writers upon the subject of glass manufacture fail to show anything decisive upon the precise period of its invention. Some suppose it to have been invented before the flood. Nervi traces its antiquity to the yet problematical time of Job.

It seems clear, however, that the art was known to the Egyptians thirty-five hundred years since; for records handed down to us in the form of paintings, hieroglyphics, &c., demonstrate its existence in the reign of the first Osirtasen, and existing relics in glass, taken from the ruins of Thebes, with hieroglyphical data, clearly place its antiquity at a point fifteen centuries prior to the time of Christ.

Mr. Kennet Loftus, the first European who has visited the ancient ruins of Warka, in Mesopotamia, writes thus: "Warka is no doubt the Erech of Scripture, the second city of Nimrod, and it is the Orchoe of the Chaldees. The mounds within the walls afford subjects of high interest to the historian; they are filled, or I may say composed, of coffins piled upon each other to the height of forty-five feet."

"The coffins are of baked clay, covered with green glaze, and embossed with the figures of warriors, &c., and within are ornaments of gold, silver, iron, copper, and *glass*."

Layard, in his discoveries among the ruins of Nineveh and Babylon, in chapter 8th, says: "In this chamber were found two entire glass bowls, with fragments of others. The glass, like all others that come from the ruins, is covered with pearly scales, which, on being removed, leave prismatic, opal-like colors of the greatest brilliancy, showing, under different lights, the most varied tints. This is a well-known effect of age, arising from the decomposition of certain component parts of the glass. These bowls are probably of the same period as the small bottle found in the ruins of the northwest palace during the previous excavations, and now in the British Museum. On this highly interesting relic is the name of Sargon, with his title of King of Assyria, in cuneiform characters, and the figure of a lion. We are therefore able to fix its date to the latter part of the seventh century B. C. It is consequently the most ancient known specimen of *transparent* glass."

In chapters 22d and 25th, he gives us the form of many glass vessels from the mound of Babel, similar in form to the modern fish-globes, flower-vases and table water-bottles of the present day — the latter being reeded must have been formed in metallic moulds — and pieces of glass tubes, the exterior impression exactly like our modern patch diamond figure.

Of the several specimens of glass brought to England by Mr. Layard, one, the fragment of a vase, when examined, was of a dull green color, as though incrusted with carbonate of copper. This color was quite superficial, and the glass itself was opaque and of a vermilion tint, attributed to suboxide of copper. The outer green covering was due to the action of the atmosphere on the surface of the glass, and the consequent change of the suboxide into green carbonate of copper. This specimen is interesting, as showing the early use and knowledge of suboxide of copper as a stain or coloring agent for glass. The ancients employed several substances in their glass, and colored glazes for bricks and pottery, but of which there remains no published record. But these glasses and other ancient works of art prove that they were familiar with the use of oxide of lead as a flux in their vitreous glasses, and with stannic acid and Naples yellow as stains or pigments.

Other writers believe that glass was in more general use in the ancient than in comparatively modern times, and affirm that among the Egyptians it was used even as material for coffins. It is certainly true that so well did the Egyptians understand the art, that they excelled in the imitation of precious stones, and were well acquainted with the metallic oxides used in coloring glass; and the specimens of their skill, still preserved in the British Museum and in private collections, prove the great skill and ingenuity of their workmen in mosaic similar in appearance to the modern paper-weights. Among the specimens of Egyptian glass still existing is a fragment representing a lion in bas-relief, well executed and anatomically correct. Other specimens are found inscribed with Arabic characters.

All writers agree that the glass-houses in Alexandria, in Egypt, were highly celebrated for the ingenuity and skill of their workmen, and the extent of their manufactures.

Strabo relates that the Emperor Hadrian received from an Egyptian priest a number of glass cups in mosaic, sparkling with every color, and deemed of such rare value that they were used only on great festivals.

The tombs at Thebes, the ruins of Pompeii and Herculaneum, and the remains of the villa of the Emperor Tiberius, go not only incidentally to establish the antiquity of the art, but also prove the exquisite taste and skill of the artists of their various periods.

The first glass-houses, well authenticated, were erected in the city of Tyre. Modern writers upon the subject generally refer to Pliny in establishing the fact that the Phœnicians were the inventors of the art of glass-making. The tradition is that the art was originally brought to light under the following circumstances. A vessel being driven by a storm to take shelter at the mouth of the river Belus, the crew were obliged to remain there some length of time. In the process of cooking, a fire was made upon the ground, whereon was abundance of the herb "kale." That plant burning to ashes, the saline properties became incorporated with the sand. This causing vitrification, the compound now called glass was the result. The fact becoming known, the inhabitants of Tyre and Sidon essayed the work, and brought the new invention into practical use. This is the tradition: but modern science demonstrates the false philosophy, if not the incorrectness, of Pliny's account; and modern manufacturers will readily detect the error, from the impossibility of melting silex and soda by the heat necessary for the ordinary boiling purposes.

It is a well-authenticated fact, however, that there were whole streets in Tyre entirely occupied by glass-works; and history makes no mention of any works of this character at an earlier period than the time mentioned by Pliny.

That Tyre possessed peculiar advantages for the manufacture, is very clear from geographical and geological data, the sand upon the shore at the mouth of the river Belus being pure silica, and well adapted to the manufacture. The extensive range of Tyrian commerce, too, gave ample facilities for the exportation and sale of the staple; and for some ages it must have constituted almost the only article, or at least the prominent article, of trade. Doubtless the rich freights of "the ships of Tyre," mentioned in Scripture, may in part have been composed of a material now as common as any of its original elements.

From Tyre and Sidon the art was transferred to Rome. Pliny states it flourished most extensively during the reign of Tiberius, entire streets of the city being then occupied by the glass manufactories. From the period of Tiberius the progress of the art seems more definite and marked, both as relates to the quantity and mode of manufacture.

It was during the reign of Nero, so far as we can discover, that the first perfectly clear glass, resembling crystal, was manufactured. Pliny states that Nero, for two cups of ordinary size, with handles, gave six thousand sestertia, equal in our currency to about two hundred and fifty thousand dollars; and that rich articles of glass were in such general use among the wealthy Romans as almost to supersede articles of gold and silver. The art, however, at that period, seems to have been entirely devoted to articles of luxury, and from the great price paid, supported many establishments,—all however evidently upon a comparatively small scale, and confined, as it would appear, to families.

Up to this period, no evidence appears to prove that any other than colored articles in glass-ware were made. It is clear, too, that the furnaces and melting-pots then in use were of very limited capacity, the latter being of crucible shape; and it was not until the time of Nero that the discovery was made that muffled crucibles or pots, as at the present day, were required in order to make crystal glass. (Without them, it is well known, crystal glass cannot be perfected.) It appears, further, that a definite street in the city of Rome was assigned to the manufacturers of this article; and that in the reign of Severus they had attained such a position, and accumulated wealth to such a degree, that a formal tax was levied upon them. Some writers take the ground that this assessment was the primary cause of the transfer of the manufacture to other places.

That the peculiar property of the manufacture at this period was its clear and crystal appearance is abundantly evident; and this, and the great degree of perfection to which the manufacture of white or crystal-like glass was carried, are by many writers thought to have been proved from classical sources,— Horace and Virgil both referring to it, the one speaking of its beautiful lustre and brilliancy, the other comparing it to the clearness of the waters of the Fucine Lake.

The decline of this art in Rome is clearly defined by various writers; and its gradual introduction into Bohemia and Venice is plainly marked out. At this latter place the art flourished to a remarkable degree, and being marked by constant progress and improvement, enabled Venice to supply the world without a rival, and with the beautiful manufacture called "Venice drinking-cups." The beauty and value of these are abundantly testified to by many authors, among whom is Holinshed, referred to previously. The manufacture of these and similar articles were located, as stated in the "Chronicles," at Murano, a place about one mile from the city, where the business was carried on, and assumed a high position in the order of the arts. And from thence we are enabled to date its future progress and gradual introduction into Europe, Germany, England, and the Western World.

It is not strange that the strict secrecy with which the business was conducted in these times, should have invested the art with an air of romance; and legends, probably invented for the purpose, created a maximum of wonder among the uninitiated. The government of Venice also added, by its course, to the popular notions regarding the high mystery of the art, conferring, as it did, the title of " Gentleman " (no idle title in those days) on all who became accomplished in the manufacture. Howell, in his " Familiar Letters," dated from Venice in 1621, says : " Not without reason, it being a rare kind of knowledge and chemistry, to transmute the dull bodies of dust and sand, for they are the only ingredients, to such pellucid, dainty body, as we see crystal glass is."

That the art had greatly improved in the hands of the Venetian artisans cannot be doubted. The manufacture was carried to a degree far beyond any previous period ; and the more so, because sustained by the governmental protection and patronage. Venice being then in the height of her commercial glory, she herself being " Queen of the Sea," ample facilities existed for the exportation of her manufactures to every part of the known world ; and for a long period she held the monopoly of supplying the cities of Europe with crystal glass in its various departments of ornament and utility.

A French writer, who published an elaborate work in twelve books upon the subject of glass manufacture, after it had been introduced into France, gives an interesting account of the rise and progress of the art in that country, the encouragement it received, and the high estimation in which it was held. After stating that it was introduced into France from Venice, he says: —

"The workmen who are employed in this noble art are all gentlemen, for they admit none but such. They have obtained many large privileges, the principal whereof is to work themselves, without derogating from their nobility. Those who obtained these privileges first were gentlemen by birth; and their privilege running, that they may exercise this art without derogating from their nobility, as a sufficient proof of it, which has been confirmed by all our kings; and in all inquiries that have been made into counterfeit nobilities, never was any one attainted who enjoyed these privileges, having always maintained their honor down to their posterity."

Baron Von Lowhen states, in his "Analysis of Nobility in its Origin," that, "So useful were the glass-makers at one period in Venice, and so considerable the revenue accruing to the republic from their manufacture, that, to encourage the men engaged in it to remain in Murano, the Senate made them all Burgesses of Venice, and allowed nobles to marry their daughters; whereas, if a nobleman marries the daughter of any other tradesman, the issue is not reputed noble."

From this statement a valuable lesson can be drawn, viz., that a strict parallel is constantly observable between the progress of this art and the intellectual and social elevation of its possessors.

Those engaged in it now do not indeed occupy the same social position; still it is probable that in foreign lands the blood of noble ancestors still runs in their veins; and even in our own democratical land, with all the tendencies of its institutions, workers in glass claim a distinctive rank and character among the trades; and in the prices of labor, and the estimate of the comparative skill involved, are not controlled by those laws of labor and compensation which govern most other mechanical professions; and similarity of taste and habit is in a degree characteristic of the modern artisan in this department, as in the case of those who, for their accomplishment in the art, were ennobled in the more remote period of its progress. The same writer says:—

"It must be owned those great and continual heats, which those gentlemen are exposed to from their furnaces, are prejudicial to their health; for, coming in at their mouths, it attacks their lungs and dries them up, whence most part are pale and short-lived, by reason of the diseases of the heart and breast, which the fire causes; which makes Libarius say, 'they were of weak and infirm bodies, thirsty, and easily made drunk,'— this writer says, this is their true character: but I will say this in their favor, that this character is not general, having known several without this fault."

Such was the character and habits of noble glass-makers four hundred years since; and whether their descendants still retain their blood or not, the habit of drinking, believed at that time necessary as consequent upon the nature of the employment, is, at the present day, confined to the ignorant, dissolute, and unambitious workmen. The habit will, doubtless, ere long be done away. Still, so long as the workmen of the present day cling to their conventional rules,— act as one body, the lazy controlling the efforts of the more intelligent and industrious,—so long will the conduct of the dissolute few affect the moral reputation of the entire body. They must not forget the old adage, that "One bad sheep taints the whole flock." The spirit of the age in no degree tends to sustain the old saying, that "Live horses must draw the dead ones."

The writer already referred to, dwelling with great interest upon the social position of those then engaged in the art, goes on to say:—

"Anthony de Brossard, Lord of St. Martin and St. Brice, gentleman to Charles d'Artois, Count of Eu, a prince of noble blood royal, finding this art so considerable, that understanding it did not derogate from their nobility, obtained a grant in the year 1453 to establish a glass-house in his country, with prohibition of any other, and several other privileges he had annexed to it. The family and extraction of this Sieur de Brossard was considerable enough to bring him here as an example. The right of making glass being so honorable, since the elder sons of the family of Brossard left it off, the younger have taken it up, and continue it to this day. Messieurs de Caqueray, also gentlemen of ancient extraction, obtained a right of glass-making, which one of their ancestors contracted by marriage in the year 1468, with a daughter of Anthony de Brossard, Lord of St. Martin, that gentleman giving half of his right for part of her fortune, which was afterwards confirmed in the Chamber of Accounts. Messieurs Valliant, an ancient family of gentlemen, also obtained a grant of a glass-house for recompense of their services, and for arms a

Poignard d'Or on azure, which agrees with their name and tried valor. Besides these families, who still continue to exercise this art, there are the Messieurs de Virgille, who have a grant for a little glass-house. Messieurs de la Mairie, de Suqrie, de Bougard, and several others, have been confirmed in their nobility during the late search in the year 1667.

"We have, moreover, in France, several great families, sprung from gentlemen glass-makers who have left the trade, among whom some have been honored with the purple and the highest dignities and offices."

Enough is recorded to show in what estimation the art was held in France by the government and people of that period; and it is in nowise wonderful that an art invested with so much distinction, conducted with so much secrecy, and characterized with so great a degree of romantic interest, should have given rise to strange reports and legends, hereafter to be referred to.

The writer referred to above states that there were two modes of manufacturing glass. One he denominates that of the "Great Glass-Houses," the other the "Small Glass-Houses." In the large houses the manufacture of window-glass, and bottles for wine or other liquors, was carried on. He states: —

"The gentlemen of the Great Glass-Houses work only twelve hours, but that without resting, as in the little ones, and always standing and naked. The work passes through three hands. First, the gentlemen apprentices gather the glass and prepare the same. It is then handed to the second gentlemen, who are more advanced in the art. Then the master gentleman takes it, and makes it perfect by blowing it. In the little glass-houses, where they make coach-glasses drinking-glasses, crystals, dishes, cups, bottles, and such like sort of vessels, the gentlemen labor but six hours together, and then more come and take their places, and after they have labored the same time they give places to the first; and thus they work night and day, the same workmen successively, as long as the furnace is in a good condition."

Every glass-maker will perceive, from the foregoing description, that the same system prevails at the present time, as to the division of labor and period of labor, so far at least as "blown articles" are concerned. The names, too, then given to glass-makers' tools are retained to the present day, and, with slight difference, the shapes of the various tools are the same.

At the best, the manufacturers of glass in France were for a long period much inferior to the Venetians and Bohemians; but after the introduction of window-glass, from Venice, the making of crystal glass greatly extended and correspondingly improved.

In the year 1665 the government of France, desirous of introducing the manufacture of window-glass, offered sufficient inducement in money and privileges to a number of French artists (who had acquired the process at Murano, at Venice) to establish works at Tourtanville. At these works the same system of blowing was followed as that used in the Venetian glass-works. A workman, under this system, named Thevart, discovered the art of casting plate-glass, and obtained from the government a patent for the term of thirty years. He erected extensive works in Paris, and succeeded in what was then deemed an extraordinary feat, casting plates eighty-four inches by fifty inches, thereby exciting unbounded admiration.

The credit of the invention of casting plates of glass belongs to France, and the mode then adopted exists at the present day, with but slight variation. France monopolized the manufacture over one hundred years before it was introduced into any other country.

Writers generally agree that the manufacture of glass was introduced into England in the year 1557. "Friars' Hall," as stated by one writer, was converted into a manufactory of window-glass,—other writers say, for crystal glass, (called by the English "flint," from the fact of the use of flint-stones, which, by great labor, they burnt and ground.) In 1575, Friars' Hall Glass-Works, with forty thousand billets of wood, were destroyed by fire.

In 1635, seventy-eight years after the art was introduced into England, Sir Robert Mansell introduced the use of coal fuel instead of wood, and obtained from the English government the monopoly of importing the fine Venetian drinking-glasses, an evidence that the art in England was confined as yet to the coarser articles. Indeed, it was not until the reign of William III. that the art of making Venetian drinking-vessels was brought into perfection,—quite a century after the art was introduced into England; an evidence of the slow progress made by the art in that country.

As France was indebted to Venice for her

workmen, so also was England indebted to the same source. Howell, in one of his "Familiar Letters," directed to Sir Robert Mansell, Vice-Admiral of England, says: "Soon as I came to Venice, I applied myself to dispatch your business according to instruction, and Mr. Seymour was ready to contribute his best furtherance. These two Italians are the best gentlemen workmen that ever blew crystal. One is allied to Antonio Miotte, the other is cousin to Maralao."

Although Sir Robert procured workmen from Venice, they were probably of an inferior character, and a space of fifty years elapsed before the English manufactories equalled the Venetian and French in the quality of their articles.

Evelyn, in his "Diary," states: "On the proclamation of James II., in the market-place of Bromley, by the sheriff of Kent, the commander of the Kentish troops, two of the King's trumpeters, and other officers, drank the King's health in a flint wine-glass three feet tall."

In the year 1670, the Duke of Buckingham became the patron of the art in England, and greatly improved the quality and style of the flint-glass, by procuring, at great personal expense, a number of Venetian artists, whom he persuaded to settle in London. From this period, *i. e.*, about the commencement of the eighteenth century, the English glass manufactories, aided by the liberal bounties granted them in cash upon all glass exported by them or sold for export, became powerful and successful rivals of the Venetian and the French manufactories in foreign markets. The clear bounty granted on each **pound of** glass exported from England, which the government paid to the manufacturer, was not derived from any tax by impost or excise previously laid, for **all such** were returned to the manufacturer, together with the bounty referred to; thereby lessening **the** actual cost of the manufacture from twenty-five to fifty per **cent.**, and enabling **the** English exporters **to** drive off all competition in foreign markets. This bounty provision was annulled during **the** Premiership of Sir **Robert** Peel, together with **all** the excise duty on **the** home consumption.

In 1673 the first plate-glass was manufactured at Lambeth, under a royal charter; **but no** great progress was made at that time, and the works for the purpose were doubtless very limited. One hundred years later, *i. e.* 1773, a Company was formed, under a royal charter, called the "Governor and Company of the British Cast Plate-Glass Manufactory," with a capital of eighty shares of five hundred pounds each, their works being at Ravenshead, in Lancashire. These works have been very successfully conducted, and, according to a late writer, are rivalled by none, excepting those at "St. Gobain," in France. Since the excise duty on plate-glass has been repealed, its manufacture has increased to a wonderful extent; the quantity used in the construction of the Crystal Palace, for the World's Fair, being probably many times larger than that manufactured twenty years since in the kingdom of Great Britain in any one year.

An English paper states that Roger Bacon, at sixty-four years of age, was imprisoned ten years for making concave and convex glasses, and camera-obscura and burning-glasses.

It is to many persons matter of great surprise that the manufacture of plate-glass has never been introduced into this country. The whole process is a simple one. The materials are as cheap here as in England or in France. Machinery for the polishing of the surface is as easily procured, and water-power quite as abundant, as in either country. The manufacture, with the materials so ready to the hand, and these together with the skill, labor, and demand, increasing every year, is most certain to realize a fair remunerating profit and steady sale. Besseman has lately introduced a new method of casting plate-glass, which, should it equal the inventor's expectation, will reduce the cost, supersede the old plan, and eventually, of course, increase the consumption.

CURIOSITIES OF GLASS-MAKING.

We gather from the ancient writers on glass-making, that the workers in the article had, at a very early period, arrived at so great a degree of proficiency and skill as to more than rival, even before the period of the Christian era, anything within the range of more modern art. The numerous specimens of their workmanship, still preserved in the public institutions of Europe, and in the cabinets of the curious, prove that the art of combining, coloring, gilding, and engraving glass was perfected by the ancients. Indeed, in fancy coloring, mosaic, and mock gems or precious stones, the art of the ancients has never been excelled. Among the numerous specimens it is remarkable that all vessels are round; none of ancient date are yet found of any other form. And no specimen of crystal glass of ancient date has yet been found.

Among the numerous antiques yet preserved,

the " Portland Vase " must hold the first place. Pellat, in his work on the incrustation of glass, states : " The most celebrated antique glass vase is that which was during more than two centuries the principal ornament of the Barberini Palace, and which is now known as the 'Portland Vase.' It was found about the middle of the sixteenth century, enclosed in a marble sarcophagus within a sepulchral chamber, under the Monte del Garno, two and a half miles from Rome, in the road to Frascati. It is ornamented with white opaque figures in bas-relief upon a dark blue transparent ground. The subject has not heretofore received a satisfactory elucidation, but the design and more especially the execution are admirable. The whole of the blue ground, or at least the part below the handles, must have originally been covered with white enamel, out of which the figures have been sculptured in the style of a cameo, with most astonishing skill and labor." The estimation in which the ancient specimens of glass were held, is demonstrated by the fact that the Duchess of Portland became the purchaser of the celebrated vase which bears her name, at a price exceeding nine thousand dollars, and bore away the prize from numerous competitors. The late Mr. Wedgewood was permitted to take a mould from the vase, at a cost of twenty-five hundred dollars, and he disposed of many copies, in his rich china, at a price of two hundred and fifty dollars each.

The next specimen of importance is the vase exhumed at Pompeii in 1839, which is now at the Museum at Naples. It is about twelve inches high, eight inches in width, and of the same style of manufacture with the "Portland Vase." It is covered with figures in bas-relief raised out of a delicate white opaque glass, overlaying a transparent dark blue ground, the figures being executed in the style of cameo engraving. To effect this, the manufacturer must have possessed the art of coating a body of transparent blue glass with an equal thickness of enamel or opal-colored glass. The difficulty of tempering the two bodies of glass with different specific gravities, in order that they may stand the work of the sculptor, is well known by modern glass-makers. This specimen is considered by some to be the work of Roman artists; by others it is thought to be of the Grecian school. As a work of art it ranks next to the "Portland Vase," and the figures and foliage, all elegant and expressive, and representative of the season of harvest, demonstrate most fully the great artistic merit of the designer.

THE ROYAL CLARENCE VASE.

William Hone, in his " Day-Book " for 1831, says, " This superb glass vase, designed by John Gunby, and exhibited at the Queen's Bazaar, Oxford Street, London, is an immense basin of copper, and its iron shaft or foot clothed with two thousand four hundred pieces of glass, construct a vase fourteen feet high and twelve feet wide across the brim, weighing upwards of eight tons, and capable of holding eight pipes of wine. Each piece of glass is richly cut with mathematical precision and beautifully colored; the colors are gold, ruby, emerald, &c.; the colored pieces being cemented upon the metal body and rendered air-tight. The exterior is a gem-like surface of inconceivable splendor; on a summer afternoon it forms a mass of brilliancy. The vase, by illumination of gas alone, glittered like diamonds upon melted gold. Mr. Reingale says the human mind, in all of its extensive range of thought, is not able to conceive a splendid glass vase cut in a more elaborate and novel way. At the first sight one is confounded with astonishment, and knows not whether what we see is real, or whether on a sudden we have not been transported to another globe. To England is due the honor of its production, and it comes from the hands of one of its numerous celebrated artists, Mr. Gunby. The precious metal, gold, glitters in all its glory, intermixed, or rather united with extraordinary beauty of cutting and rich and splendid enamelled painting. One is at a loss whether most to admire the shape, the gorgeous brilliancy, the sparkle of the gems, the beauty of the cutting, the enamelling, the general conception, or the immense bulk of this magnificent and astounding work of art."

The "Scientific American" states, "The troup of glass-blowers at Hope Chapel furnish a very interesting evening's entertainment for those who are fond of practical things. A steam-engine, most beautifully constructed of different colored glass, is worked by steam all the time. The nature of the material affords an opportunity to see all the several parts moving at once, and it is really a very curious sight, even to an engineer, and one that will well repay a visit."

Among the numerous specimens of ancient glass now in the British Museum, there are enough of the Egyptian and Roman manufacture to impress us with profound respect for the art as pursued by the earlier workers in glass. Among them is a fragment considered as the *ne plus ultra* of the chemical and manipulatory skill of the ancient workers. It is described as consisting of no less than five layers or strata of glass, the interior layer being of the usual blue color, with green and red coatings, and each strata separated from and contrasted with the others by layers of white enamel, skilfully arranged by some eminent artist of the Grecian school. The subject is a female reposing upon a couch, executed in the highest style of art. It presents a fine specimen of gem engraving. Among the articles made of common material are a few green vases about fifteen inches high, in an excellent state of preservation, and beautiful specimens of workmanship. In the formation of the double handles and curves, these vases evince a degree of skill unattained by the glass-blowers of the present period.

The cases in the Egyptian room at the Museum contain several necklaces, small figures, scarabæi, and other objects, which would appear to an ordinary observer to be composed of precious stones. They are, in fact, at least most of them, formed either of glass throughout the whole substance, or of materials covered with a glass coating. The manufacture of articles of this description presupposes a market for them ;

and the desire upon the part of the less affluent members of society to possess, at a cheap rate, ornaments in imitation of their superiors, necessarily leads to the conclusion that, even at the most ancient of the periods I have mentioned, the Egyptians had made a remarkable advance in the customs of civilized life. The Museum cases also exhibit networks of glass bugles, with which the wrappers of mummies were often decorated; and there is abundance of evidence to show that wine was frequently served at table in glass bottles and cups. Alexander the Great is said to have been buried at Alexandria in a coffin composed wholly of glass.

The specimens taken from the tombs at Thebes are also numerous. Their rich and varied colors are proofs of the chemical and inventive skill of the ancients. These specimens embrace not only rich gems and mosaic work, but also fine examples of the lachrymatory vase. Some of the vases are made from common materials, with very great skill and taste. The specimen of glass coin, with hieroglyphical characters, must not be omitted; as also a miniature effigy of the Egyptian idol "Isis"; a specimen of which proves that the Egyptians must have been acquainted with the art of *pressing* hot glass into metallic moulds, an art which has been considered of modern invention. English glass-makers considered the patent pillar glass a modern invention until a Roman vase was found (it is now to be seen in the Polytechnic Institution in London), being a complete specimen of pillar moulding. Pillat states in his work that he had seen an ancient drinking vessel of a Medrecan form, on a foot of considerable substance, nearly entire, and procured from Rome, which had the appearance of having been blown in an open-and-shut mould, the rim being afterwards cut off and polished. This is high authority, and, with other evidences that might be cited, goes far to prove that the ancients used moulds for pressing, and also for blowing moulded articles, similar to those now in use.

Pompeian window-glass, of which panes have been discovered as large as twenty by twenty-eight inches, has proved, on examination, to have been cast in a manner similar to that now followed in making plate-glass, except that it was not rolled flat, as now, by metal cylinders, but pressed out with a wooden mallet, so that its thickness is not uniform.

A glass has been discovered at Pompeii, about the size of a crown piece, with a convexity, which

leads one to suppose it to be a magnifying lens.
Now, it has been said that the ancients were not
aware of this power, and the invention is given
to Galileo by some, to a Dutchman, in 1621, by
others, while a compound microscope is attributed
to one Fontana, in the seventeenth century. But
without a magnifying glass, how did the Greeks
and Romans work those fine gems which the human eye is unable to read without the assistance
of a glass? There is one in the Naples Royal
Collection, for example, the legend of which it
is impossible to make out, unless by applying a
magnifying power. The glass in question, with
a stone ready cut and polished for engraving,
are now to be seen in the Museum of Naples.

Specimens of colored glass, pressed in beautiful forms for brooches, rings, beads, and similar
ornaments, are numerous. Of those of Roman
production many specimens have been found in
England. Some of these were taken from the
Roman barrows. In Wales glass rings have
been found; they were vulgarly called " snake
stones," from the popular notion that they were
produced by snakes, but were in fact rings used
by the Druids as a charm with which to impose
upon the superstitious. We find, too, that the
specific gravity of the specimens referred to

ranges from 2034 to 3100, proving oxide of lead to have been used in their manufacture; the mean gravity of modern flint-glass being 3200.

From what we gather from the foregoing facts, we are inclined to the belief that, in fine fancy work, in colors, and in the imitation of gems, the ancient glass-makers excelled the modern ones. They were also acquainted with the art of making and using moulds for blown and pressed glass, and forming what in England is now called patent pillar glass. All these operations, however, were evidently on a very limited scale, their views being mainly directed to the production of small but costly articles. Although in the time of the Roman manufacturers vases of extra size were made, requiring larger crucibles and furnaces than those used by the glass-makers of Tyre, yet it is evident that they produced few articles except such as were held sacred for sepulchral purposes, or designed for luxury. And while they possessed the knowledge of the use of moulds to press and blow glass by expansion, it does not appear that they produced any articles for domestic use. If it were not thus, some evidences would be found among the various specimens which have been preserved.

LEGENDS OF THE GLASS-HOUSE, ETC.

Enough has been adduced to show the peculiar estimation in which the art of glass-making was formerly held, and the privileges conferred on it by the various governments of Europe.

The art was thus almost invested with an air of romance; and a manufacture commanding so much attention on the part of the governments was regarded with a great share of awe and wonder.

It is not strange that, in this state of things, various legends should have been identified with the manufacture and its localities. Among these legends was that which ascribed to the furnace-fire the property of creating the monster called the Salamander. It was believed, too, that at certain times this wonderful being issued from his abode, and, as opportunity offered, carried back some victim to his fiery bed. The absence of workmen, who sometimes departed secretly for foreign lands, was always accounted for by the hypothesis that in some unguarded moment they had fallen a prey to the Salamander. Visitors, too, whose courage could sustain them, were directed to look through the bye-hole to the interior of the furnace, and no one failed to discover the monster coiled in his glowing bed, and glaring with fiery eyes upon the intruder, much to his discomfiture, and effectually as to his retreat. Some gallant knights, armed *cap-a-pie*, it is said, dared a combat with the fiery dragon, but always returned defeated; the important fact being doubtless then unknown or overlooked, that steel armor, being a rapid conductor of heat, would be likely to tempt a more ready approach of the fabled monster.

There was another current notion, that glass was as easily rendered malleable as brittle, but that the workmen concealed the art, and the life of any one attempting the discovery was surely forfeited. An ancient writer on glass, " Isidorus," states that, in the reign of Tiberius, an artist, banished from Rome on political considerations, in his retirement discovered the art of rendering glass malleable; he ventured to return to Rome, in hopes of procuring a remission of his sentence, and a reward for his invention; the glass-makers, supposing their interest to be at stake, employed so powerful an influence with the Emperor (who was made to believe that the value of gold might be diminished by the discovery), that he caused the artist to be beheaded, and his secret died with him. " Blancourt" relates that, as late as the time of Louis XIII., an inventor having presented to Cardinal Richelieu a specimen of malleable glass of his own manufacture, he was rewarded by a sentence of perpetual imprisonment, lest the "vested interest" of French glass manufacturers might be injured by the discovery. Even at the present day the error is a popular one, that if the art of making glass malleable were made known, it would have the effect of closing nearly all the existing glass-works; while the truth is, that quite the reverse would be the result. Whenever the art of making glass malleable is made known, it will assuredly multiply the manufacture to a tenfold degree.

It was formerly the custom for the workmen, in setting pots in the glass-furnace, to protect themselves from the heat by dressing in the skins of wild animals from head to foot; to this "outre" garb were added glass goggle-eyes, and thus the most hideous-looking monsters were readily presented to the eye. Show was then made of themselves in the neighborhood, to the infinite alarm of children, old women, and others. This always occurred, with other mysterious doings, on the occasion of setting the pot, or any other important movement attendant on the business. The ground was thus furnished for very much of the horrible *diablerie* connected with the whole history of the manufacture.

A belief was long prevalent that glass drinking vessels, made under certain astronomical influences, would certainly fly to pieces if any poisonous liquid was placed in them; and sales of vessels of this kind were made at enormous prices. Another idea pervaded the community, that vessels of a certain form, made in a peculiar state of the atmosphere, and after midnight, would allow a pure diamond to pass directly through the bottom of the vessel. Various articles, such as colored goblets, were thought to add to the flavor of wine, and to detract materially from its intoxicating quality.

All these, and many other popular notions, added greatly to the mystery and renown of glass manufacturers. We close this number with an extract from "Howell's Familiar Letters." "Murano," says he, "a little island about one mile from Venice, is the place where crystal glass is made, and it is a rare sight to see whole streets where on one side there are twenty furnaces at work. They say here, that although one should transfer a furnace from Murano to Venice, or to any of the little assembled islands about here, or to any other part of the earth beside, to use the same materials, the same workmen, the same fuel, and the selfsame ingredients every way, yet they cannot make crystal glass in that perfection for beauty and lustre as at Murano. Some impute it to the circumambient air, which is purified and attenuated by the concurrence of so many fires, that are in these furnaces night and day perpetually, for they are like the vestal fires, never going out."

There is no manufacturing business carried on by man combining so many inherent contingencies, as that of the working of flint glass. There is none demanding more untiring vigilance on the part of the daily superintendent, or requiring so much ability and interest in the work. Unlike all other branches of labor, it is carried on by night and day, is governed by no motive power connected with steam or water, and has no analogy to the production of labor by looms or machinery.

The crude material of earth being used, each portion requires careful refining from natural impurities, and when compounded, being dependent upon combustion in the furnace for its completion, (which combustion is effected by change of the atmosphere beyond the power of man to direct, but exercises a power to affect the heat of the furnace acting for good or for evil,) much responsibility rests upon the furnace-tenders; constant care on their part is required. A slight neglect affects the quality of the glass. A check upon the furnace in founding-time will spoil every pot of metal for the best work. Overheat, too, will destroy the pots, and the entire weekly melt will be launched into the cave, at a loss of several thousand dollars. Even with the utmost care, a rush of air will not uncommonly pass through the furnace and destroy one or more pots in a minute's space. And when the furnace has yielded a full melt, and is ready for work, many evils are at hand, and among the ever-jarring materials of a glass-house, some one becomes adverse to a full week's work; vigilance is not always the price of success.

Again: no branch of mechanical labor possesses more of attraction for the eye of the stranger or the curious, than is to be witnessed in a glass-house in full play. The crowded and beelike movements of the workmen, with irons and hot metal, yet each, like the spheres of his own orbit, presents a scene apparently of inextricable confusion.

It is a difficult task to describe the curious and interesting operations of the glass-blowers; for the present we may say, that there is no other employment so largely dependent upon steadiness of nerve and calm self-possession. The power of manipulation is the result of long experience. The business of the glass-blower is literally at his "fingers' ends." It is most interesting to witness the progress of his labor, from the first gathering of the liquid metal from the pot, and the passing it from hand to hand, until the shapeless and apparently uncontrollable mass is converted into some elegant article. Equally interesting is it to witness with what dexterity he commands, and with what entire ease he controls the melted mass; the care, also, with which he swings it with force just enough to give it the desired length, joins it to other pieces, or with shears cuts it with the same ease as paper. The whole process, indeed, is one filled with the most fascinating interest and power.

Of all the articles of glass manufacture, none command a greater degree of attention than the article called the salver, and no other develops so pleasing and surprising effects in its processes. When seen for the first time, the change from a shapeless mass, the force with which it flies open at the end of the process, changing in an instant into a perfect article, all combine to astonish and delight the beholder.

Mystery is as much a characteristic of the art now as at any former period; but it is a mystery unallied to superstition, — a mystery whose interpreter is science, — a mystery which, instead of repelling the curious and frightening the ignorant, now invites the inquiring and delights the unlearned.

By the following, we find that the romance of glass-making has not yet died out. We copy from the "Paris Annual of Scientific Discovery," for 1863, the following: —

"It would appear there is yet some secret in glass-making unknown to the world at large, as the manufactory of Mr. Daguet, of Soletere, France, is known to be in possession of an undivulged method, which enables them to make glass of a purity which all other manufacturers are not able to rival. A railway, recently constructed and running past Mr. Daguet's works, has so affected the glass-pots, by the tremor occasioned by the locomotives and trains, that work has had to be suspended. For this Mr. Daguet brought an action, during the past year, against the railway company for damages; but when the case came on for trial, the court held that it would be impossible to assess damages unless it were made cognizant of the secret, and its pecuniary advantage to Mr. Daguet. The latter declined imparting this, and the court refused to proceed further."

We have shown that glass, while it has contributed so largely to the material well-being of man, has also administered profusely to the pleasure of woman. The belle enjoys the reflection of her beauty in its silvered face,— a pleasure peculiarly her own, as we all know,— and if we may believe poesy, the mermaid, her rival of the coral groves in the fathomless ocean, looks with equal satisfaction upon her dubious form, as seen in her hand-mirror. And what would Cinderella be to the nursery without her glass slipper!

But leaving poetry to its own prolific devices, where would science find itself without the aid of glass? The astronomer's and chemist's vocation would be gone. Suns, planets, and stars would have no exact existence to us, and their laws be unknown. The seaman would blunder his way on the ocean, lucky if he guessed aright his course, and cursing his "stars," when he did not. In short, glass is the indispensable servant of science in almost all its forms, and where it does not discover it protects. Its loss would throw back the world into antediluvian ignorance, not to mention the countless eyes it would deprive of sight, of their intellectual food, and freedom of way.

MANUFACTURE OF GLASS IN THE UNITED STATES, ETC.

The last number of our series of articles upon this highly interesting subject — interesting both as concerns the various features of the manufacture, and as indicative of the progress of the art in the successive ages of the world's history — closed the sketch of the rise and progress of the manufacture of flint glass. Our sketch has covered the ground so far as time would allow, from the introduction of the art into Egypt, through its transfer to Tyre and Sidon, and from thence, in its order, to Rome, Venice, France, and finally into England.

The reader will notice that this progress, like that of many others, is almost identical, for a time at least, with the gradual extension of conquest, and especially with this, as connected with the extension of the Roman sway.

We now reach the period of its introduction

into the Western continent, and propose giving an outline of its gradual extension and characteristics in our own land.

Our opportunity of research as to the period of the introduction of glass manufacture into this country, induce the belief that the first effort was made some years before the American Revolution.

This attempt was by a company of Germans, who selected the town of Quincy, in this State, as the place in which to establish the manufacture.

We are acquainted with little beyond the fact, that such an attempt was made; their success, or the length of time during which they carried on the work, are matters equally beyond our knowledge. Some specimens of their articles still exist, showing mainly that they engaged in the manufacture of what is called black metal only; these also are of the rudest style of the art.

The place in Quincy in which their manufactory was established acquired the name from them of "Germantown," which name it retains to the present time. The site of their manufactory is now occupied, we believe, by the institution called "The Sailors' Snug Harbor."

A Connecticut paper states a patent was

granted by that State, in 1747, for twenty years, to Thomas Darling, for the exclusive privilege of making glass. This Act appears to have become void, because of the patentee not fulfilling its conditions, and at various times after this special grants were made to others to introduce the manufacture of glass.

The Historical Society of Brooklyn, N. Y., has in their cabinet "a glass bottle, the first one manufactured at a glass-works started, in 1754, near the site of the present glass-works in State Street. This enterprise, we are informed, was brought to an untimely end for want of sand, — that is, the right kind of sand." From this we infer, it must be a flint-glass bottle, as the sand suitable for green or black glass abounds on their shore.

Shortly after the close of the Revolutionary struggle, we think about the year 1785, the late Robert Hewes, a well-known citizen of Boston, made, probably, the first attempt to establish a window-glass manufactory on this continent. This manufactory was modelled upon the German system. Mr. Hewes carried his works to the fuel, and erected his factory in the then forest of New Hampshire. The writer well remembers, when a boy, hearing Mr. Hewes relate, that when building his glass-works the tracks of bears were frequently seen in the morning in and around his works.

From the best information in our possession, we think that to Mr. Robert Hewes must be conceded the first attempt to establish window-glass making in the United States, or in the western world. The aim of Mr. Hewes was doubtless to supply the most important and necessary article made of glass, and called for by the immediate wants of the people, viz., window-glass. It ended, however, in disappointment to the projector, probably from the frequent error of carrying such works into the interior, to the vicinity of fuel, or from lack of skill on the part of the workmen.

This attempt was followed, about the year 1787, by Messrs. Whalley, Hunnewell, and their associates, and by the workmen Plumback and Cooper, who erected a large factory in Essex Street, Boston (where Edinboro' Street now is), for the purpose of making the Crown Window Glass. This was without success, until a German, of the name of Lint, arrived in the year 1803, and from this period there was great success in the manufacture, for the State of Massachusetts, to encourage the manufacture of window-glass, paid the proprietors a bounty on every table of glass made by them. This was done to counteract the effect of the bounty paid by England on the exportation of glass from that kingdom. The State bounty had the effect to encourage the proprietors and sustain their efforts, so that by perseverance many difficulties were overcome, and a well-earned reputation supported for the strength and clearness of their glass; a glass superior to the imported, and well known throughout the United States as " Boston Window-Glass." This reputation they steadily sustained, until they made glass in their new works at South Boston, in the year 1822. Their charter from the State was highly favorable to the stockholders; among the privileges it granted an exclusive right to manufacture for fifteen years, and to manufacture glass without their consent subjected the offender to a fine of five hundred dollars for each offence. Their capital was exempt from taxation for five years, and the workmen exempted from military duty.

From the founding of this establishment may be dated the founding of all the Crown and Cylinder, Window and Flint Glass-Works in the Atlantic States. Indeed, this may be considered the fruitful parent tree of the many branches now so widely spread abroad.

The wonderful mystery attached to the art of glass-making seems to have followed its introduction into this country. The glass-blower was considered a magician, and myriads visited the newly-erected works, and coming away with a somewhat improved idea of an unmentionable place and its occupants; and the man who could compound the materials to make glass was looked upon as an alchemist who could transmute base metal into pure gold.

The fame of the works spread into a neighboring State, and in 1810 or 1811 a company was formed in Utica, to establish glass-works in that place, and quite a number of workmen in the Essex Street Works were induced to leave their employ and break their indentures from the offer of increased wages; while, however, on their way, and just before they reached the State line, they, with the agent, were arrested, brought back, and expensive lawsuits incurred. The Utica Works were abandoned, and, we believe, never revived.

Subsequently another company was formed in New York, being influenced by a fallacious view of the silicious sand. This company erected their works at Sandy Lake, a locality abounding both in silex and fuel. A few years' trial convinced the proprietors the place was ill chosen, and, after the experience of heavy losses, it was abandoned.

A Doctor Adams, of Richmond, Virginia, made large offers of increased wages to the workmen of the Essex Street Works, who were then induced to abandon their place of work and violate their indentures. They succeeded in reaching Richmond to try their fortune under the auspices of the Doctor. A few years' experience convinced them of the fallacy of increased pay; for, after very heavy losses, the works were abandoned and the workmen thrown out of employ. The proprietors of the Essex Street Works had engaged workmen in the mean time, at a very heavy expense, from England — a most difficult task, for the English government made it a penal offence to entice workmen to leave the kingdom at that period.

In 1811 the proprietors of the Essex Street Works erected large and improved works on the shore at South Boston. To supply the workmen enticed away, and also to meet the wants of their factory, an agent was sent to England to procure a set of glass-workers. By the time they reached this country the war with England broke out, and the enterprise was thus defeated; for it became difficult to procure fuel and the various means for carrying on the Essex Street Works.

The making of window-glass in Boston led to the introduction of the manufacture of flint-glass, arising from the excess of window-glass blowers, brought into the country by the enterprise of the Boston Window-Glass Company; many among the number from Europe had worked more or less in flint-glass works (no unusual thing in England), for a good flint-glass blower, with manual strength, can fill the part of a window-glass blower, and exceedingly well.

Among the number was a Mr. Thomas Caines, now living at South Boston, having retired from the business with an independent property, the honest fruit of his skill and industry; he may be truly considered as the father of the flint-glass business in the Atlantic States.

Mr. Caines proved competent to the task, not only as a first-rate workman, but possessed the art of mixing the materials and being able to sustain all the other departments appertaining to the business. He prevailed upon the proprietors to erect a small six-pot flint furnace in part of their large unoccupied manufactory in South Boston.

At that time the articles of flint-glass imported

by the earthenware trade were confined to a very few articles, such as German straw tumblers, cruets, salts, and plain decanters of cheap fabric; of the finer articles, to cut finger tumblers, sham diamond cut dishes, and Rodney decanters; a quality of glass and cutting that would not at the present day command one-fifth of their then cost.

War having interrupted the importation of glass, the manufactory supplied the then limited demand, and gave full employ for their factory.

Contemporaneous with the South Boston enterprise, a company was formed and incorporated under the title of the Porcelain and Glass Manufacturing Company. Their factory was located at East Cambridge, then called Craigie's Point. Their china department was directed by a Mr. Bruitan, but for want of proper materials it proved an entire failure. Their glass-works were under the direction of a Mr. Thompson, who built a small six-pot furnace, similar in size to the one at South Boston. Thompson brought out a set of hands, at a heavy expense, to work the furnace, but the result proved he was in no way qualified for the task, nor possessed of the least practical skill or knowledge of the business, and of course proving an entire failure. The attempt to make porcelain and glass was abandoned by the company.

In 1815, some of the workmen left the South Boston Factory and hired of the Porcelain Company their six-pot furnace, and commenced the making of flint-glass under the firm of Emmet, Fisher & Flowers. They succeeded for a time very well, and turned out glass suitable for the trade; but want of concert of action prevented a successful result, and they dissolved without loss. The Porcelain Company, discouraged by so many failures, agreed to wind up their concern, and in November, 1817, they disposed of their entire property at public auction.

As one manufactory dies out only to give place to another, so the present New England Glass Company was formed, and became the purchasers of the Porcelain Works. That company, from 1817, to the present time, have pursued the business with signal success; beginning with the small capital of forty thousand dollars, they have from time to time increased it, until it amounts at the present time to half a million of dollars. They commenced business with a small six-pot furnace, holding seven hundred pounds to each pot; employed, all told, about forty hands, and the yearly product did not exceed forty thousand dollars. They now run five furnaces, averaging ten pots to each, capacity of two thousand pounds to each pot. They employ over five hundred men and boys, and the yearly product is not less than five hundred thousand dollars.

In 1820 some of their workmen left them, built a factory in New York City, and conducted their business under the firm of Fisher & Gillerland. In 1823 Gillerland dissolved the connection and built, on his own account, a manufactory in Brooklyn, N. Y., which he conducts at this period with great skill and success, and is considered the best metal mixer in the United States.

In 1825 a Flint-Glass Manufactory was established by individual enterprise in Sandwich, Mass. Ground was broke in April, dwellings for the workmen built, and manufactory completed; and on the 4th day of July, 1825, they commenced blowing glass — three months from first breaking ground. In the following year it was purchased of the proprietor, a company formed, and incorporated under the title of Boston and Sandwich Glass Company. Like their predecessors, they commenced in a small way; beginning with an eight-pot furnace, each holding eight hundred pounds. The weekly melts at that period did not exceed seven thousand pounds, and yearly product seventy-five thousand dollars; giving employment to from sixty to seventy hands. From time to time, as their business warranted, they increased their capital until it reached the present sum of four hundred thousand dollars. Their weekly melts have increased from seven thousand pounds to much over one hundred thousand pounds; their hands employed from seventy to over five hundred; their one furnace of eight pots to four furnaces of ten pots; and yearly product from seventy-five thousand dollars to six hundred thousand dollars.

In 1820 another secession of workmen from the New England Glass Company took place, to embark on their own account their savings of many years in the doubtful enterprise of establishing flint-glass works in Kensington, Philadelphia, under the title of the Union Flint-Glass Company. The proprietors, being all workmen, were enthusiastic in the project, happy in the belief that they could carry it on successfully, work when convenient, and enjoy much leisure. All was *then* to them sunshine. Ere long they realized the many inherent evils attendant on flint-glass works; the demon of discord appeared among them, and they discovered, when too late, that they had left a place of comfort and ease for a doubtful enterprise. Death thinned their ranks, and the works, after passing into other hands for a short trial, have years since ceased to exist.

From 1820 to 1840 very many attempts were made, by corporations and firms, to establish the manufacture of flint-glass in the Atlantic States, but almost with entire failure. The parent tree, the old South Boston concern, failed; the works were revived from time to time by at least five different concerns, and all ended in failure; and for years the works remained closed, till the present occupant, Mr. Patrick Slane, hired the premises, and by his enterprise and great industry has greatly enlarged the works, and is now carrying on a large and active business. In his factory we learn the old system among the operatives he does not allow to have a foothold, and the individual industry of his hands is not cramped or limited by the oppressive system of the old school operative.

As a record of the past and a reference for the future, we find, in reviewing the various attempts to establish flint-glass works in the Atlantic States, that it would not be just to place the names of those identified with them before the reader; for many were deluded by the projectors with promises of the most flattering success, but realized only disappointment and loss.

In enumerating all the concerns, companies, and corporations that have been engaged in the manufacture of flint-glass in the Atlantic States, we find the number to be forty-two; of which number two concerns have retired, and ten are now in operation, viz., two at East Cambridge, three at South Boston, one at Sandwich, three near New York City, and one at Philadelphia; leaving two concerns who retired with property, and twenty-eight out of the forty-two concerns entire failures, involving the parties interested in heavy loss, the fate of the existing ten to be determined by future events.

Before closing, we may allude to the repeated failure of permanently establishing window- and bottle-glass works in this vicinity. The primary cause has been in the construction of the furnaces, no improvement for centuries having taken place, but the old defective plan being adhered to by workmen from Europe. A casual observer must see they are defective, and consume double the quantity of fuel really required for the weekly melts. The rate of wages for experienced workmen, about threefold over the German rates, has heretofore checked success, but at the present time is more than compensated by machinery and materials.

The manufacture of plate-glass offers a profitable and inviting field that should be improved. The consumption in this country is large and increasing yearly. Materials are cheaper than in Europe, and as the most essential part is performed by machinery and motive power, this will more than equalize the extra rate of wages that may be taxed upon a new undertaking.

We have recorded the rise and progress of the Glass Manufacture in the Atlantic States, showing its course from its introduction in 1812 to the present period, *i. e.* 1852, covering a space of time of just forty years.

We now turn to the introduction of the manufacture in the Western States, for the account of which we are indebted to Mr. Thomas Bakewell, of Pittsburg, Penn. Mr. Bakewell advises us, that, prior to the year 1808, glass-works were established by a company of Germans, near Fredericktown, Maryland, under the direct control of a Mr. Amelong, for the purpose of manufacturing glass in all its branches. We have not ascertained the precise year in which Mr. Amelong commenced the manufacture; but previous to the year 1808 the establishment was broken up, and the workmen dispersed. Most of them reached Pittsburg, Penn., and a part of them were engaged by Col. James O'Hara, in the establishment of the first window-glass factory in the Western States. The same factory is in operation to the present day, and others of the Fredericktown company were instrumental in introducing the same branch of the glass business into Pennsylvania, at New Geneva, upon the property of the late Albert Gallatin. Others of the number, previously mentioned, established themselves in Baltimore, and in all of the places noticed. Some of their descendants still continue the business.

There are at this time ten window-glass factories in the vicinity of Pittsburg, and fifteen in the river towns, — in all twenty-five works, — manufacturing over 220,000 boxes of window-glass of 100 feet each annually.

We now proceed to examine a more interesting topic, viz., the rise and progress of the flint-glass business in the West. We have shown that most of the workmen, on the breaking up of the glass-works in Fredericktown, migrated to Pittsburg, attracted there, doubtless, by the coal mines. Some of these persons were successful in establishing the manufacture of window-glass, while a portion of the workmen, in the spring of the year 1808, attempted to establish a flint-glass manufactory upon part of the premises now occupied by Bakewell & Pears, extensive flint-glass manufacturers. The persons engaged in the enterprise, however, were deficient, both in the requisite knowledge and capital; the effort proved abortive, the parties quarrelled, and the establishment, in an incomplete condition, was offered for sale.

In the August following, a Mr. Bakewell and his friend, Mr. Page, being on a visit to Pittsburg, were induced to purchase the concern, under the representation of one of the owners that he possessed the information and skill requisite for the proper pursuit of the business, having been engaged (as he stated) in the business before he left England. Mr. Bakewell had scarcely entered upon his new pursuit before he discovered that the qualification of the person alluded to had been entirely misrepresented, and that to succeed he must rely upon his own experience and diligence in the attainment of the peculiar knowledge indispensable to the success of his undertaking. In this the fortune of his family and friend were, of course, deeply involved, and he therefore set himself to the accomplishment of his task most manfully. Those only who have practical experience of the character of the undertaking can fully appreciate the various and almost insurmountable difficulties to be encountered and overcome before success could be attained.

His first difficulty arose from want of skill in the workmen, and the inferiority of the materials employed in the manufacture of flint-glass. So little were the resources of the West developed at that day, that Mr. Bakewell had to procure his pearlash and red lead from Philadelphia, the pot clay from Burlington, N. J.,— the whole being transported over the mountains in wagons to Pittsburg. The only sand then known was the yellow kind, obtained in the vicinity, and used at this time only for window-glass. For many years Mr. Bakewell obtained the saltpetre needed from the caves of Kentucky, in a crude state, which article he was obliged to purify, until the period of 1815, when the required supply was obtained from Calcutta.

The few workmen then in the country were not well instructed in the making of glass articles, after the glass was prepared, to which was added the great evil (which has too usually prevailed among the imported workmen) of a determination to prevent the instruction of apprentices by the most arbitrary and unjust means, and, so far as it was in their power, endeavoring to prevent competition, by not only controlling the hours of work, but the quantity of manufacture; in fact, doing the least amount of work possible for the largest amount of pay that could be coerced from the proprietors. Experience, however, showed Mr. Bakewell how to construct his furnaces, or, at least, to improve on the old; and he discovered better materials in his immediate vicinity, and succeeded in making purer glass than he had before made. The oppressive acts of the workmen, in the mean time, compelled Mr. Bakewell to resort to England for new workmen, at a time when the prohibitory laws there in regard to mechanics leaving England were in full force, — an undertaking requiring great secrecy, and at the risk of long imprisonment if detected.

Such were some of the embarrassing circumstances with which Mr. Bakewell had to contend. Of the full force and extent of these, those only can conceive who have been under like necessities and circumstances. But a brighter day was dawning upon his exertions, and at length his arduous and untiring labor was crowned with the desired success. Good clay was procured from Holland, and purer materials discovered; competent workmen were either imported or instructed, and the flint-glass manufacture was firmly established at Pittsburg. From this first establishment there originated, in a few years, many other glass-works, erected chiefly by persons who had acquired the art with Mr. Bakewell, or had obtained the requisite means while in his employ. We may well consider Mr. Bakewell as the father of the flint-glass business in this country; for he commenced the work in 1808, and by untiring efforts and industry brought it to a successful issue.

For the skill, judgment, labor, and perseverance devoted by him to the progress of the art, he truly merits the "Artium Magister" so often bestowed on those least worthy of its dignity and honor. Theory in Science too often receives the meed which practical progress in its walks so richly deserves. Mr. Bakewell lived to realize an ample fortune as the fruit of his industry, and his sons still carry on a profitable business on the premises originally occupied by their father. By father and sons this has covered a space of forty-four years, a length of time rarely finding a business in the same family in America. May the factory be always occupied and conducted by a Bakewell.

The furnace built by Mr. Bakewell in 1808 contained only six pots, twenty inches in diameter, which were replaced in 1810 by a ten-pot furnace of a larger capacity, and in 1814 another furnace was added to the works, of like capacity.

In 1809 another concern sprung up, and carried on the business on a limited scale; in 1812 another succeeded, making three concerns carrying on the business; and in 1810 another company was formed, but failed in a few years.

There are now in Pittsburg nine concerns manufacturing flint-glass, running thirteen furnaces and one hundred and five pots. There are also three concerns at Wheeling, running five furnaces and forty-five pots. There are also at Wellsville, Steubenville, and Cincinnati one or two factories each, besides several manufactories for green glass jars, and one for the making of porter bottles; one also for mineral-water bottles.

The first glass-cutting works were opened in 1809 by a German of the name of Echbaum, who had settled in Pittsburg some years previously. Mr. Bakewell also carried on glass-cutting, and among his workmen was an Englishman who had served as a soldier in Canada, being taken as a prisoner in one of the battles on the Lakes in 1813. He proved not only a good glass-cutter, but an excellent mechanic, in various branches; but still a dissipated and idle man, and of course of but little service in the manufactory.

One of the amusing incidents connected with the manufacture occurred when General Clark (then Governor of Missouri) took a party of Osage Chiefs to Washington. On their way they visited Bakewell's Glass-Works, and their attention was greatly excited; they watched with great curiosity the process of making various articles, and the mode of affixing the handle to a glass pitcher quite disturbed the equanimity of the head chief, who, after shaking hands with the workmen, said, through the interpreter, "That man must have had some intercourse with the Great Spirit."

The following, from Sigma's pen, shows a decanter-stopper can be made to point a moral or illustrate a satire:—" Mr. Flint, in his 'Ten Years in the Valley of the Mississippi,' tells a pleasant story of an Indian who told him he had *big diamond*, for which he had given trader *much beaver*. A time was appointed, and Mr. Flint visited the wigwam to examine the diamond, which, after considerable mystery, was brought forth from its place of concealment, and proved to be a broken glass decanter-stopper. When an individual, eminent for his talents and learning, has been justly decorated with the degree of LL.D., and finds the same mark of distinction bestowed upon others who are remarkable for neither, he cannot fail to perceive an amusing resemblance between his diploma and Kunkerpot's diamond."

IMITATION OF MUSLIN-GLASS.

Here is a simple and ingenious means of giving to glass the appearance of delicately wrought muslin: —

The process, which comes to us from Germany, consists in spreading very smoothly a piece of lace or tulle, and covering it with some fatty substance by means of a printer's roller. The glass being carefully cleaned, the cloth is laid upon it so as to leave in fat a print on the surface of all the threads of the fabric. The glass is then exposed about five minutes to the vapors of hydrofluoric acid, which roughens the spaces between the lines, and leaves the polish on the surface under the fat.

A glass thus prepared becomes like a veil, protecting from exterior indiscretion persons who, from their apartment, desire to look commodiously outside.

We recall here that the manipulation of hydrofluoric acid requires great prudence. This acid is so corrosive that a drop of its vapor condensed produces upon the hand a lively inflammation, and may even lead to graver accidents. Breathing the emanations should therefore be avoided with the greatest care.

No art has been characterized, in the course of its progress, by so much of wonder and undefined belief in the supernatural, as that of the manufacture of glass in its various modes and articles.

The old glass-works in Wellsburg, Va., were pulled down a few years since with a tremendous crash. They were erected in 1816, and, with the exception of the establishments at Pittsburg, were the oldest west of the mountains. The beginning of their career was prosperous, but the last owners have invariably sunk money in carrying on the works, and to prevent further losses they have now been finally destroyed, and the ground turned into a potato-patch.

[From the "Scientific American."]

ETCHING AND ORNAMENTING GLASS.

The hardest glass may be etched and frosted with a peculiar liquid acid, and also with this acid in the condition of vapor. When powdered fluor spar is heated with concentrated sulphuric acid in a platinum or a lead retort, and connected with a refrigerator by a tube of lead, a very volatile, colorless liquid is obtained, which emits copious white and suffocating fumes. This is hydrofluoric acid, a dilute solution of which attacks glass with avidity, while neither sulphuric, nitric, nor muriatic acid has the least effect upon it. In a diluted state it is employed for glass etching, for which purpose it is kept in a lead vessel, because it has very little affinity for this metal. The vapor of this acid is also used for the same purpose. The glass to be operated upon is first coated with a ground of wax, and the design to be etched is then traced through the wax with a sharp instrument. In a shallow lead basin some powdered fluor spar is then placed, and a sufficient quantity of sulphuric acid poured upon it to convert it into a thin paste. The glass to be etched is now placed in the basin, to which a gentle heat is applied, when the vapor of the acid is disengaged and attacks the traced lines from which the wax has been removed. The operation is completed in a few minutes, the glass is removed, and the wax cleaned off with warm oil of turpentine. All those parts which have remained covered with the wax are now clear as before, while the other parts drawn by lines to represent figures have a frosted appearance. Any person can produce figures on glass with this acid, but, for reasons before stated, it is dangerous to use.

In October, 1859, a patent was granted to James Napier, of Glasgow, Scotland, for a very simple method of ornamenting glass with fluoric acid. Instead of drawing patterns and figures on the glass with the use of varnish and a graver to prepare the glass for etching, the glass is prepared by simply transferring pictures from prints, which can be performed by almost any person. The method is, to take a print, lithograph, or picture made with printer's ink, and fix the printed surface to the glass by any ordinary paste made from starch. All the air must be carefully excluded from between the print and glass. When perfectly dry, liquid hydrofluoric acid about the specific gravity of 1.14 is applied for about three minutes, when it is washed in water to remove the paper and the acid, and the figure of the print is then found upon the glass. The printed portion of the paper may also be cut in outline and pasted on the glass, then transferred. Glass that is "flashed" on the surface with another color may be treated in this manner, when a portion of the flashing or surface will be removed, and the picture will remain in color.

COLORED GLASS.

The distinguished French chemist, M. Chevreul, who has devoted so much attention to the subject of color, has lately published a memoir on painted windows, in which there are many points which deserve the attention of artists and others who are interested in the manufacture of colored glass. It has often been much noticed that old stained glass windows have a much richer effect than modern ones, and M. Chevreul, speaking of this superiority, attributes it to what moderns regard as defects. In the first place, much of the ancient glass is of unequal thickness, and so presents convex and concave parts, which refract the light differently and produce an agreeable effect. In the next place the old colored glass is not a colorless glass, to which has been added the particular coloring material, such as protoxide of cobalt, &c. Old glass contains a good deal of oxide of iron, which colors it green, and to this must be attributed the peculiar effects of antique glass, colored by cobalt and manganese. M. Chevreul appears to think that modern stained glass is too transparent to produce the best effects. M. Regnault, the chemist, has recommended that all this kind of stained glass should be cast, to avoid the monotonous effect of plain surfaces on the light; and also that foreign substances should be mixed with the glass to diminish its transparency.

Many attempts have been made to color with ruby or other colors gas shades, so as to throw on surrounding objects the color of the glass; but in no case has the ray of light passing through colored glass, to refract the shade, been successful.

But when a ray of solar light is passed

through a colorless prism, it is refracted, and forms, when thrown on a wall or screen, a broad band of colored light, — red, orange, yellow, green, blue, indigo, and violet,— which is known as the prismatic or solar spectrum.

ARTIFICIAL DIAMONDS.

We find a report in French journals that M. Gannal has succeeded in obtaining *crystals*, having all the property of the diamond, through the mutual reaction of phosphorus water and bisulphide of carbon upon each other for the space of fifteen weeks.

The crystals were found to be so hard that no file would act upon them. They cut glass like ordinary diamonds, and scratched the hardest steel. In brilliancy and transparency they were in no way inferior to the best jewels, and some possessed a lustre surpassing that of most real stones.

For reference we record the cost of materials for flint-glass, say in 1840 to 1845, as follows: —

Litherage, or red lead, cost .	$6\frac{1}{2}$ cts. per lb.	
Pearlash, ...	6 "	"
Nitre, ...	6 "	"
Silex, ...	$0\frac{1}{2}$ "	"

Present price, 1864: —

Red lead,	. . . .	21 cts. per lb.
Pearlash,	. . . .	17 " "
Nitre,	. . . .	6 " "
Silex,	. . . .	0¾ " "

We now refer to the early introduction of the manufacture of glass into England. The English manufacturers, like ourselves, had to struggle with the various evils incident to the introduction of a new art. France and Germany, from their long experience in the making of glass, were enabled for a long time to undersell the English manufacturer in his **own market.**

To foster and protect this branch of national industry, **the** English **government** imposed a **heavy** tax on all **foreign** glass imported into their dominions. This measure secured to the English manufacturer the entire trade, both with **their** colonies and with the home market, thus giving such substantial encouragement to the enterprise, that, in a few years, the manufacture was so much increased as to admit of exportation.

To stimulate the exportation **of** various articles of English production, the government, in the latter part of the eighteenth century, granted bounties, from time to time, on linens, printed cottons, glass, &c., &c. Until the bounty on glass was allowed, the exportation of glass from England to foreign countries was very limited; for the French and Germans, as has before been stated, for various reasons could undersell the English; but the government bounty changed the aspect of affairs, and shortly the English manufacturers not only competed with the Germans and French for the foreign market, but actually excluded them from any participation,— the government bounty being equal to one half the actual cost of the glass exported.

An Act of Parliament levied on flint-glass an excise duty of ninety-eight shillings sterling on all glass made in England, which excise was paid by the manufacturer, being about twenty-five cents per pound weight, without regard to quality; but if such glass was exported, the excise officer repaid the tax which it was presumed the manufacturers had paid, and a clear bounty of twenty-one shillings sterling was paid by the government to the exporter on each hundred weight of flint-glass shipped from England, being equal to five cents per pound. Under such encouragement the export increased from year to year to a very great extent, so that the excise duty of ninety-eight shillings sterling on the amount consumed at home did not equal the amount paid out in bounty. In the year 1812, fifty-second George III., an Act was passed reducing the excise duty to forty-nine shillings, and the export bounty to ten shillings sixpence. In 1815 the Act was renewed, and again in 1816. In 1825, sixth George IV. chap. 117, an Act was passed revising the former as to the mode of levying the excise duty and bounty, so as to prevent frauds on the revenue, which had hitherto been practised to a very great extent. This act remained in force until the Premiership of Sir Robert Peel, when both excise and bounty were abrogated, and the English manufacture stands on the same footing in foreign countries as those of other nations. By the protecting hand of the English government the flint-glass manufactories multiplied with very great rapidity, underselling all other nations, and not only rivalling, but far excelling them in the beauty, brilliancy, and density of the articles manufactured.

The greatest stimulus ever given to the glass manufacture of England was the abolition of the duty on it in 1845. That abolition has produced a somewhat paradoxical result. While the quantity of glass made has increased in the proportion of three to one, the number of manufacturing firms has diminished in the proportion of one to two. In 1844 there were fourteen companies engaged in the manufacture. In 1846 and 1847, following the repeal of the duty, the number had increased to twenty-four. The glass trade, after the removal of the heavy burden imposed upon it, seemed to offer a fair opening for money seeking investment. The demand for glass was so great that the manufacturers were in despair. Glass-houses sprang up like mushrooms. Joint-stock companies were established to satisfy the universal craving for window-panes. And what was the result? Of the four-and-twenty companies existing in the year 1847, there were left, in 1854, but ten. At this time there are but seven in the whole United Kingdom. Two established in Ireland have ceased to exist. In Scotland, the Dumbarton Works, once famous, were closed in 1831, by the death of one of the partners, afterwards reopened, and again closed. The seven now existing are all English.

The manufacture of the finer kinds of glass was introduced into England not many years ago from Germany, and German operatives were employed at very high wages. We understand that the English glass is now superior to the German.

There is only one plate-glass factory in the United States. It was commenced only two years ago near New York, and we understand that it has met with encouraging success.

Soon after the introduction of the business into this country, a very great improvement in the mode of manufacture was introduced. Pallat, in his admirable work on glass, alludes to the American invention in only a few words, and passes it by as of but slight importance; but it has brought about a very great change, and is destined to exert a still greater; in fact, it has revolutionized the whole system of the flint-glass manufacture, simply by mould machines for the purpose of pressing glass into any form. It is well known that glass in its melted state is not in the least degree malleable, but its ductility is next to that of gold, and by steady pressure it can be forced into any shape. The writer has in his possession the first tumbler made by machinery in this or any other country. Great improvement has of course taken place in the machinery, insomuch that articles now turned out by this process so closely resemble cut-glass that the practised eye only can detect the difference.

Still, the entire field of improvement is not occupied, and greater advances will yet be made. The tendency, in this particular, has been so to reduce the cost of glass that it has multiplied the consumption at least tenfold; and there can be no reasonable doubt but that, at this period, a much larger quantity of flint-glass is made in this country than in England. The materials composing glass are all of native production, and may be considered as from the earth. The pig lead used is all obtained from the mines in the Western States; ashes from various sources in other States; and silex is also indigenous. The materials consumed yearly, in the manufacture, are something near the following estimate:—

Coal, for fuel,	48,000 tons;
Silex,	6,500 "
Ash, Nitre, &c.,	2,500 "
Lead,	3,800 "

for the flint manufacture. How much more is consumed by the window-glass manufacturers, the writer is without data to determine.

We have recorded the progress of improvement in the manufacture of glass, and now, relevant to the subject, we propose to examine the various improvements in working furnaces and glass-houses. To this end we present to our readers the drawing of a furnace for flint-glass,[1] with the interior of a glass-house as used by the Venetians, at the highest point of the art, in the sixteenth century.

The workmen in glass will see, that, as compared with the factories of the present day, the Venetians in their instrumentalities were subjected to many difficulties, — they were oppressed by the furnace smoke, and in no way protected from the heat of the furnace, or enabled to breathe fresh atmospheric air; in fact, the impression prevailed in those days that the external air, drawn into the glass-house, was detrimental to the business, and therefore it was most cautiously guarded against.

The drawing is taken from an ancient work on glass, and although limited in the view, shows the general plan. The factory wall was conical, and rose like a large chimney, with a few windows for the admission of light. Exposed to the heat of the summer sun of Venice, and of the furnace within, neither the comfort nor health of the workman was secured. The construction of the annealing department shows two tiers of pans, the use of which must have been attended with great loss of materials.

[1] See drawing No. 1, at end of book.

Yet, with all the perceptible inconvenience, no material change in construction was made for centuries. The same plan was adopted in France and England, and it is only within the present century that any change has taken place in the latter country. In fact, in the year 1827 an Englishman erected a glass factory on the same plan in the vicinity of New York, which, from its defective construction for this climate, soon passed out of use.

The Germans, however, departed from the Venetian plan so far as to place the furnace in a large and well-ventilated building, but without a furnace-cone to carry off the heat and smoke; still a decided improvement was thus effected over the system in use in France and England.

The plan referred to shows to the practical workmen of the present day the excessive waste of fuel arising from the construction of the furnace; for the same expenditure of fuel in the American furnace would melt ten times the material produced from the Venetian.

It is admitted that the American glass-house is far in advance of the European ones at the present day, in the particulars of capacity, ventilation, comfort of the workmen, and economy in fuel. An impression is very prevalent that glass-making is an unhealthy occupation. It may have been thus in former times; but, as a matter of fact, no mechanical employment is more healthy. Dissipated as glass-makers have been in former days, and careless of their health as they are at present, no better evidence can be adduced to prove the *generally* healthy character of the employment than the fact that the Glass Manufacturing Company in Sandwich, averaging in their employment three hundred hands, had not a man sick through the influence of the employment, or one die in their connection, for the space of twenty years.

Drawing No. 2[1] represents the plan adopted in the French flint-glass furnaces. These at one period were worked by noblemen only, — the labor of the furnace-tender and taker-in being performed by servants, as before stated. The apparel and general style of dress, as indicated by the drawing, shows that more attention was paid to the fashion of the day than to comfort. The form of the furnace being similar to the Venetian shows it to have been subject to the same unnecessary waste of fuel; but it would appear that the French manufacturers had taken one step towards improvement, in using the waste fuel of the furnace to anneal their glass. The

[1] See drawing No. 2, at end of book.

Venetians had a separate furnace to anneal their glass, supported by independent fires, as used at the present day. The place marked D, over the crown of the furnace, is the door of the annealing oven; but the drawing is so imperfect that the artist does not show by what flues the smoke escapes, or in what way the glass was drawn from the annealing oven; for only the external view of the furnace is given. But it is fair to presume that the plan was the same as still exists in France, and as adopted by a French company now working a flint-glass factory in Williamsburg, near New York; viz., — the taker-in, so called, mounts by steps to door D and places the articles in iron pans, which are slowly drawn over the furnace and through another door on the opposite side, to allow the glass vessels to cool gradually. The use of this plan is sustained by writers who describe the tools used to carry the glass articles into the upper oven to cool. In connection with the drawings of the ancient glass-furnaces, we deem it proper to give a drawing of glass-makers' tools [1] in use at that period, so that the glass-makers of the present day may observe with what instruments their noble predecessors in the art performed their labor.

[1] See drawing No. 3, at end of book.

In many of these tools we perceive the same general characters as mark those in use now. In some, improvements have been effected; while others are quite obsolete. It is quite curious to observe the etymology of many of the technical terms of the art in use at the present day. The name of the present polished iron table, *i. e.* the MARVER, is derived from the practice of the Italians and French in using slabs of polished marble. The iron now called the *punty*, from the Italian *ponteglo*. The tool now called *percellas*, from the word *porcello*. In fact, nearly all the technical terms in the glass manufacture, appertaining to the tool or furnace, are derived from the Italian. By referring to the drawing, we see that the tool marked A is the blow-iron, that marked B the punty-iron. Their character plainly indicates that the work made on them must have been confined to small or light articles. C, the scissors, D, the shears, correspond to those used at the present day. The tool marked E was used to finish part of their work. F and G were their large and small ladles,— the small used to take off the then called alkalic salt, showing that they were troubled with an excess of this in their time. The shovel, then called stockle, marked H, was used to carry glass articles to the annealing oven, forks not being then in use. The crooked iron I was used to stir up the metal in the pots. The tool L was used to form or hold large articles, their punty-iron not having sufficient strength. The tool M was used to carry flat articles to the annealing ovens. The tool N was used in refining their alkalic salts, and served to take off the salt as crystallized in course of its manufacture. The workmen of the present day will see that, as before remarked, many tools are not altered in form, while in others there is a decided improvement, — in none more than in the tool E. Tool D is exactly like those now in use; but many new tools have been introduced since that period, rendering most of the old tools useless. Improvements in the form of glass-furnaces, construction of the glass-house, tools, &c., have been very gradual, — more so, in fact, than in almost any other art, when we consider that a period of about four hundred years has elapsed since the furnaces, tools, &c., herein referred to, were in use, and that they remained very much the same until the present century. It is indeed no undue arrogance of claim to say that the very many improvements in furnaces, working machinery, tools, &c. (such as enable the manufacturer here to melt with the same fuel double the quantity of glass that can at present be done in the European furnaces,) are entirely owing to the progress of the art in this country. By the perfection of our machines double the product can be obtained; and although the glass-maker is paid at least three times the wages usually paid in Germany or France, we can, in all the articles where the value of the materials predominates, compete successfully with importers of foreign glass, but when the labor on glass constitutes its chief value, then glass can be imported cheaper than it can be manufactured in this country. Essentially, however, we may say, in the realm of art as in that of civilization and progress,—

"Westward the star of empire takes its way."

PRESSED GLASS.

This important branch of glass-making demands more than a passing notice. Although it is commonly believed here that the invention originated in this country, the claim cannot be fully sustained. Fifty years back the writer imported from Holland salts made by being pressed in metalic moulds, and from England glass candlesticks and table centre-bowls, plain, with

pressed square feet, rudely made, somewhat after
the present mode of moulding glass. From 1814
to 1838, no improvement was made in Europe
in this process, which was confined to common
salts and square feet.

America can claim the credit of great improvements in the needful machinery which has advanced the art to its present perfection. More
than three quarters of the weekly melt is now
worked up into pressed glass, and it is estimated
that upwards of two million dollars has been
expended in the moulds and machines now used
in this particular branch of glass-making. This
leaves Europe far behind us in this respect.
With us there is active competition for excellence. It is, however, conceded that James B.
Lyon & Co., of Pittsburg, stand first. To
such a degree of delicacy and fineness have they
carried their manufacture, that only experts in
the trade can distinguish between their straw
stem wines, and other light and beautiful articles
made in moulds, and those blown by the most
skilled workmen. When we consider the difference in the cost between pressed and blown
ware, this rivalry in beauty of the former with
the latter becomes all the more important to the
public, as it cheapens one of the staple necessaries of civilized life.

Great credit therefore is due this firm for their success in overcoming difficulties well understood by glass-makers, and doing away with the prejudice of the skilled blowers, who naturally were not inclined to put the new and more mechanical process of manufacturing glass on a par with the handicraft of the old. Lyon & Co. also excel all other American firms in large ware for table services, as well as in the more delicate objects of use.

In speaking of the improvements in glass-making in America, we must not overlook what has been done by the New England Glass Company.

Convinced of the importance of scientific skill in their business, they secured some years ago the services of Mr. Leighton and his three sons, at a liberal compensation. Besides possessing the best practical knowledge, they had also artistic taste, which enabled them to give elegant finish to their workmanship, and to introduce new and more beautiful patterns into it.

They did not neglect, however, the more homely but useful articles; but executed orders for large and heavy objects for druggists' and chemical wares and philosophical apparatus, so satisfactorily as to secure a monopoly in them.

Their richly cut, gilded, colored, and ornamental glass is considered equal to European work.

John L. Gillerland, late of the Brooklyn Glass-Works, is remarkably skilful in mixing metal. He has succeeded in producing the most brilliant glass of refractory power, which is so difficult to obtain. A gold medal was awarded his glass, in face of European competition, at the Great International Exhibition in London, 1852. In making rich glass, the gaffer or foreman must understand the science of chemistry sufficiently well to mix and purify his materials in the best possible manner, removing all crude or foreign matter, and combining the proper substances into a homogeneous mass. Without this practical experience and knowledge, his glass, instead of being clear and brilliant, and of uniform color, will be dull, and of many hues or shades. It is important also that his personal character be such as to command the respect of the workmen.

LENSES.

Optical glasses have engaged the attention and investigation of scientific men for centuries. We read of the wonderful exploits of the burning lens of Archimedes, and find the remains of lenses thousands of years old in the ruins of Nineveh, Babylon, and Pompeii. They are of the utmost importance in the science of astronomy. The slow progress made in perfecting them shows the inherent difficulties that exist in obtaining glass of the required purity. One of these is the different specific gravities of the material used. Hence the lower part of a pot of melted glass is of greater specific gravity than the top, causing a tendency to cords or threads, an evil which science has yet to learn to overcome. Not even the large bounty offered by the English Government and the Board of Longitude has been successful in effecting any important improvement in this branch of manufacture. Munich enjoys the reputation of producing the best lenses, and consequently the finest telescopes. Sir Isaac Newton, Gregory, Dolland, Keir, and others adopted lenses made from flint- and from crown-glass, it being necessary to use both in the construction of achromatic telescopes, one possessing as small and the other as great dispersive powers relative to the mean refractive powers as can be procured. But the inherent defect of the lenses still remained. M. Macquer remarks, "The correction of this fault appears therefore to be very difficult." He had tried in vain to remove it by very long fusion and fierce fire. Others have found this by experience not to correct, but to augment the evil. Mr. Keir is of opinion that some new composition must be discovered, which, along with a sufficient refractive power, shall possess a greater uniformity of texture.

Since then, it is certain some improvement has been made in the composition for lenses. In an English paper we find the following: — "One of the most remarkable optical lenses of modern manufacture is that produced by Messrs. Chance, English manufacturers, being an attempt by them to improve the manufacture of glass for optical purposes. The diameter is twenty-nine inches, and it is two inches and a quarter thick. It is really not a lens, but a plain disk intended for a lens, should its quality be sufficiently fine. The weight is about two hundred pounds. This piece of glass was inspected, on its first public exhibition, by eminent scientific judges. It was by them examined edgewise, transversely, and obliquely; it was viewed by daylight and by candle-light; it was tested by the polariscope and by other means; and after having been thus subjected to a severe ordeal, it was pronounced to be the largest and finest known specimen of the kind."

The promise held out by the foregoing we fear has failed, as in very many previous cases, or the world ere this time would have heard of its success. An achromatic object-glass for telescopes consists of at least two lenses, the one made of flint-glass, and the other of crown-glass. The former, possessing least power of dispersing the colored rays relative to its mean refractive power, must be of greater value than the latter. It is upon this principle that the achromatism of the image is produced, the different colored rays being united into one focus. Flint-glass, to be fit for this delicate purpose, must be perfectly homogeneous, of uniform density **throughout** its substance, and free from wavy veins or cords.

From the foregoing, the reader will see **that**, as has been said, the chief difficulty which exists in making telescopic lenses arises from want of pure **glass**. Every attempt to correct this evil has failed; it is well known our best telescopes and like optical **instruments** have always achromatic lenses, and for photographic purposes achromatic lenses are indispensable. If philosophers and astronomers have with so imperfect lenses attained so much, what may not the astronomer **look** for when science gives him lenses made **from** pure **glass?** If the heavens, by imperfect instruments, have so far been unveiled, to what extent may he not then be able to penetrate the pure ether, and reveal planets and heavenly bodies as yet unknown?

We close our reminiscences of Glass and its manufacture, by presenting to our readers a view of an American model glass factory of the present day.[1] By comparing this view with the sketches heretofore given of the early Venetian and French factories, they will perceive the very great improvement which is apparent over the ancient plans, an improvement conducing alike to the health and comfort of the workmen. Thirty years have passed in its development, during which many difficulties arose from the conflicting opinions of the English and German glass-makers; and, in fact, it was not until the proprietors boldly separated themselves from the current and influence of old, and almost fixed opinions, that any decided progress was shown in the development of manufacturing efficiency, or any plan contributing to the health and comfort of the workmen employed.

It is to be borne in mind that the first glass works in this country were established by the Germans, who used no other fuel than wood, the

[1] See drawing No. 4, at end of book.

furnaces for window-glass constructed under their directions being for that fuel only; on the other hand, the English workmen who introduced the making of flint-glass had made use of no other fuel than coal, and the English were therefore obliged to adopt (for the want of coal) the German plan for furnaces, and adapt the same to the making of flint-glass. The house was like the furnace, half English and half German, and from the year 1812, for thirty years, little or no improvement was made in this particular. Year after year the old plan was followed, until necessity paved the way for new plans in the effort to secure a less expensive mode of melting glass.

The result has been highly favorable. More than one half has been saved in the melt, annealing leers, and working places, yielding the workmen greater space and facilities in performing their work, and no longer exposing them to the discomfort of extra heat, smoke, and unhealthy gases. These improvements have enabled the American manufacturer to sustain his business in the severe and trying competition with foreign manufacturers, who forced their glass into this country through their agents a few years since, in such quantities, and at such reduced prices, as seriously to affect the prosperity of our artisans ; yet, aided as they have been by a tariff directly promoting foreign interest, and by the very low rates of wages paid on the Continent, they have been successfully contended with, and now a home competition has sprung up, reducing prices below a fair standard, — a competition, the result of enterprise, which will, erelong, regulate itself, for we fully hold to the maxim, that competition, honest and well sustained, is the soul and life of business: —

> " No horse so swift that he needs not another
> To keep up his speed."

There is no mechanical employment in this country yielding so good returns to the industrious as a good worker in glass, of the present day, can secure in the exercise of his skill. And we may still further say that there is no mechanical branch of industry offering such advantages for the full manifestation of a workman's real skill and industry, if the conventional usages which restrict the work could but be abrogated, — usages tending to a limited amount of work, and consequently making the workman to realize but a limited amount per week. Such workmen, of all others, should be allowed the inherent and inalienable right to work as long, and at such times, as the individual may deem for his comfort and interest.

We have expressed the opinion that the manufacture of glass is as yet but in its infancy. The experience of every day confirms the assertion, and illustrates the maxim that "life is short, art is long."

The time is not far distant when this country will become, we think, the largest exporter of glass, and the manufacture compose a most important item in every assorted export cargo. In this connection a hint to ship-owners may not be amiss. It is well known that in England, when a ship is put up for a foreign port, it is the custom to rate the freight according to the value of the merchandise,— dry goods paying the highest freight, hardware the next highest, earthen and glass ware the lowest. If our merchants would adopt this plan, very many of our bulky manufactures would find a market abroad; when, however, the same rate is required for a cask of glass ware as for a case of silks or prints, it taxes the latter a small percentage, but practically vetoes the export of the glass.

Our task is now ended; our object has been to give a simple and succinct outline of the characteristics and progress of the Glass Manufacture, to suggest such hints as might bear upon the further advance of the art, and the preservation of those practically identified with the manufacture, and, if possible, to attract the attention of those hitherto unacquainted with its nature and history. If we have neglected the maxim that "*those who live in glass houses,*" &c., it has not been from the want of honest endeavors to remember it; and if we have contributed either to the instruction or the pleasure of any reader, (and this is our hope,) we shall not regret the hours spent in the preparation of this little work.

APPENDIX.

RECEIPTS, ETC.

There are plenty of receipts for the composition of flint or crystal glass, but no mixture that we know can secure a uniform shade in each pot. The component parts of glass are well known, and the mixer's sure guide is to watch the effect of heat on each pot, for he soon finds the mixture that gives good color in one pot will in another in the same furnace prove bad. If he possesses sufficient knowledge of the chemical causes, he can correct the evil.

Among the valuable receipts for rich colors is the following, for RUBY GLASS, which takes the lead both in cost and richness : —

Take one ounce of pure gold; dissolve in a glass vessel two ounces pure sal ammoniac acid, and five ounces of pure nitric acid, which will take six to seven days ; drop in at a time say one twentieth part of the gold. When the first piece is dissolved, drop in another twentieth portion of the gold, and so on until the ounce of gold is all dissolved. This will require twenty-four hours. Evaporate the solution to dryness. Then prepare in a glass vessel six ounces pure nitric acid, two ounces muriatic acid, and one ounce of highest proof alcohol ; mix them well together, and drop in pure grained tin a bit at a time, *but beware of the fumes.* Stir it well with a glass rod ; dilute the solution with eighty times its bulk of distilled water ; then take the prepared gold, dissolved in a quart of distilled water, and pour it steadily into the solution of tin as above prepared, stirring all the while. Let it settle twenty-four to thirty hours; pour off the water, leave the settlings, pour in two thirds of a quart of water. Stir it thoroughly; let it settle thirty hours; pour off as before, and filter the precipitate through filtering paper. The result is the purple of Crassus. The ounce of gold thus prepared must be well incorporated with the following batch: say thirty-two pounds fine silex, thirty-six pounds oxide of lead, sixteen pounds refined nitre; melt the same in a clean pot, one little used, and smooth inside; when filled in, put the stopper to the pot loose, leaving it slightly open; leave it five or six hours, or time to settle, then a back stopper can be put up. In the usual time it will be ready to be worked out in solid, egg-shaped balls, and exposed to the air to be partially cooled; they are then to be placed in the leer under a strong fire, which will in two or three hours turn them to a red color; then the pans may be drawn slowly to anneal the balls.

It is well known to mixers that colored glass is derived from metallic oxides. To obtain the proper color depends on the purity and strength of the metallic oxides. The following receipts have with success been used:—

ALABASTER.

To 500 lbs. of batch add
   30 " phosphate of soda,
   10 " allumine, — *i. e.* calcined alum,
    3 " calcined magnesia.

BLACK.

To 1400 lbs. of batch add
  180 " manganese,
  100 " calcined iron scales, made fine,
   20 " powdered charcoal,
   10 " arsenic.

CANARY.

To 100 lbs. of batch add
8 ounces best oxide of uranium,
1 dr. oxide of copper.

The common colors of purple, blue, emerald, or **green**, are too well known to require to be repeated here.

The following receipt for crystal glass is on the European standard, viz.:—

1200 lbs. silex,
800 " red lead,
440 " pearlash,
50 " nitre,
10 " phosphate of lime,
10 oz. white oxide of antimony,
24 " manganese,
32 " arsenic,
20 " borax.

GERMAN SHEET GLASS.

400 lbs. silex,
130 " soda,
126 " hydrate of lime,
4 " charcoal,
7 " nitrate of soda,
4 " arsenic,
1 " manganese.

Gold-colored spangles may be diffused through the glass by mixing gold-colored tales in the batch.

AGATE.

To 150 lbs. flint batch add
10 " phosphate of lime,
6 " arsenic.

BLACK.

600 lbs. flint batch,
40 " manganese,
46 " oxide of iron.

LIGHT EMERALD GREEN.

200 lbs. flint batch,
2½ " iron filings, calcined,
½ " antimony.

ORIENTAL GREEN.

110 lbs. flint batch,
1 " oxide of uranium,
2 oz. carbonate of copper

OPAL.

500 lbs. batch,
60 " phosphate of lime,
4 " arsenic,
20 " nitrate of soda.

Said to turn without cooling.

William Gillender, of England, gives the following receipt for Bohemian Red, or Ruby:—

Sand, 62 lbs.
Lead, 76 "
Nitre, 22 "
Antimony, 8 oz.
Manganese, 3 "

Add one ounce of purple of Crassus to every eighty pounds of the above batch.

WAX RED.

To 15 lbs. flint batch add
1 " raw brass,
¾ " crocus martus.

This he says is very good.

TURQUOISE.

To 1100 lbs. flint batch add
90 " phosphate of lime,
15 " arsenic,
15 " calcined brass dust.

VIOLET.

To 100 lbs. flint batch add
1 " calcined brass,
1½ " zaffre.

Receipts for window-glass are as numerous as for flint. The following are in general use in England, so says Gilleuder:—

CROWN GLASS.

Sand, 1400 lbs.
Quick lime, 480 "
Sulphate of soda, 560 "
Charcoal, 25 "

PLATE GLASS.

Sand, 300 lbs.
Sulphate of soda, 450 "
Quick lime, 100 "
Nitre, 25 "
Charcoal, 5 "

DIAMOND GLASS.

Four pounds of borax, one pound of fine sand; reduce both to a subtile powder, and melt them together in a closed crucible set in an air furnace, under a strong fire, till fusion is perfect. Let it cool in the crucible, and a pure, hard glass, capable of cutting common glass like a diamond, which it rivals in brilliancy, is produced.

LEAD.

Lead is an important and costly ingredient of flint-glass, used as a protoxide, either as litharge or red lead, and should be perfectly pure, for the presence of any other substance or metal will be shown in the color of the glass. Consequently, the purity of the glass depends mainly on the quality of the metallic lead and its being well manufactured.

The writer believes he was the first person in the United States, aided by a director of the New England Glass Company, to build a lead furnace. This was in 1818. His only guide was a volume of "Cooper's Emporium of Arts and Sciences," which furnished a plan on a very limited scale.

The furnace proved successful, and enabled the Company to continue their manufacture of glass at a period when no foreign red lead was to be procured. They enlarged their works, until they have become the most important in the country; while for over thirty years they monopolized the business in all its branches, from the highest qualities of pure Galena and painter's red lead to common pig lead. In manufacturing metallic lead, its weight is materially increased by the absorption of oxygen gas. In 1847 the writer made many test experiments, one as follows: 660 pigs of blue lead, weighing 45,540 pounds, turned out from the ovens 48,750 pounds of litharge, — an increase in weight of 3210 pounds.

The cost of labor was $65.50; fuel, $86.50; engine power, $17.50; total, $169.50; and the market value of the excess in weight of the lead was $250, showing a satisfactory profit to the company for their outlay in this branch of their business. Chemistry gives the increase in course of manufacture: In protoxide state, 7 per cent.; in deutoxide state, 11 per cent.; in tritoxide, 15 per cent.

Muriatic acid will detect iron in lead, on dissolving a small piece of lead in the acid. If colorless, it is good.

Nitric acid will detect if there is cobalt in the lead, by adding to the acid half the quantity of high-proof alcohol. If present, the evidence is soon seen.

Some use the following as more direct: — In a small evaporating glass dish place say one ounce of lead; cover it **with muriatic acid**; dissolve the lead over a spirit lamp, add a little water, and let it settle; draw it off into another glass vessel, and add five or six drops of the solution of potash. If the lead is suitable for glass-makers, the solution will be of a light, clear, greenish color; if of a blue or purple shade, it is not suitable for flint-glass.

SAND, OR SILEX.

In the manufacture of glass it is essential that the silex should be perfectly pure, as the slightest mineral taint affects the color.

At first the New **England** factories got their sand from Demerara, brought **as ballast**, and the quality **was good**. During the War of 1812 this **source** of supply was cut off, but Plymouth beach provided **for the** wants **of the** manufacturers, **until a** better sand was discovered at **Morris River, N. J.**, though not up **to the full** requirement of the **art**. For ten years past, Berkshire **County**, Mass., has furnished sand; the best quality is owned **by G. W.** Gordon, Esq. By thorough washing, **and** passing it **through** fine sieves, and proper packing, **he now** commands the market, and delivers it ready for use. The purity has been tested, as shown by the following **extract from a** report by Professor **A. A. Hayes, M. D.**, of Boston, Massachusetts **State** Assayer, of the result of analyses of three **samples of Berkshire sand, taken from three** different locations owned by Mr. Gordon, **viz.:** —

"For the manufacture of glass, the slight amount of earth, in mica and tourmaline, contained in these samples, is **of no** account, the impurity being such oxides as color glass. **The** analyses therefore give only the proportion of coloring oxides; and, for simplicity of statement, the total weight of coloring oxide in each sample is determined in one part or **pound**.

"Sample B analyses: 4000 parts of this sample contain one part of oxide of iron.

" C analyses: 3333 parts of this sample contain one part of oxide of iron.

" P analyses: 3460 parts of this sample contain one part of oxide of iron.

"Sample B is equal in purity to the best sand known as a material for glass, in this or any other country."

FURNACES.

Next to pots, furnaces are most important for the success of a glass manufactory. Long ago it was seen that the old English plan was defective. They consumed coal at an extravagant rate, though this was not a serious drawback in England, because the furnaces were located near coal-mines, and run with a quality called slack, not otherwise merchantable. English furnaces were constructed with reference to durability, usually eight feet in diameter at the interior base, and six feet clear at the crown. This rule was followed in this country until 1840. The writer, having occasion to build an extra furnace, adopted the novel plan of one fourteen feet diameter at the base in the clear and only five feet at the crown, braced by binders, with cross-ties to prevent lateral expansion, which was a success.

A furnace on the old plan consumed 2575 bushels of coal weekly, and refined only 38,000 pounds of raw material. The new refined 35,000 pounds, with a consumption of only 2000 bushels of coal. Since then a further decrease in consumption of coal has been produced by the use of the Delano patent, which feeds the furnace by forcing up the coal at the bottom of the burning mass, thus consuming the entire smoke, and obviating the necessity of wheeling coal on the glass-house floor and impeding the workmen. It also does away with all danger to the pots in feeding the fires. Besides these great advantages, it distributes a regular and uniform heat to each **pot,** causing the pots to last much longer, and fusing the metal better, — important items to mixers.

From three to five tons **of fuel is** the weekly saving in **a** first-class furnace.

It is of vital importance to obtain pots that will last a reasonable time. **Clays** of the finest quality are essential. Each piece must **be freed from any** foreign matter, particularly sulphate of iron, which **often occurs.** The burnt and raw clay should **be well mixed, wet, and frequently kneaded, or trod over by the naked feet.** Tenacity **must** be secured, sufficient that a roll twelve to eighteen inches long can be suspended, and hold firmly together by its **own** adhesiveness. The next point is to make the pots free from air blisters, all portions being compact; then to dry them thoroughly, which requires great care on **account** of the **inequality of** the **different** parts. Pot-makers **are not agreed as to the value of different clays, and the use and proportion of raw to** burnt shells. Some use sixteen parts raw to eleven burnt, some fifty-five raw to forty-five burnt, **some equal proportions of each.**

Manufacturers have **mainly** depended upon imported clays, **but the** Western glass-makers have used Missouri clay with success. In the east it has not yet come into general use. Of the imported, that from Stowbridge is considered best. Garnkerk is a strong clay, and, if well selected, **will** rival any other. The analyses are **for**

STOWBRIDGE,

Silica, 64 parts,
Alumina, 20 "
Lime, 1 "
Iron, 3 "

GERMAN,

Silica, 46 parts,
Alumina, 34 "
Iron, 3 "

GARNKERK,

Silica,   53 parts,
Alumina, 43   "
Lime,   1   "
Iron,   1   "

FRENCH,

Silica,   40 parts,
Alumina, 31   "
Iron,   3   "

WESTERN,

Silica,   49 to 52 parts,
Alumina, 31 to 32   "
Iron,   2 to 4   "

FUEL.

This subject deserves special notice. We have said that the New England manufacturers at first used wood only, which was prepared by being split into equal lengths, with an average diameter of two inches, and then kiln-dried to dispel the sap and moisture. This fuel was supplied to the furnace at opposite fire-holes, a stick at a time, which was a laborious and heating process.

Subsequently, a furnace was built at South Boston, over a cave, and unkilned wood was used in clefts. This saved one quarter in fuel, but it used up the pots so rapidly as to prove to be no economy in the end. After the development of the Virginia coal mines, our furnaces were altered to use coal, which proved to be more convenient and less costly than wood. The Pictou and Cumberland mines also increased the supply; and at present all the furnaces in New England, with one exception, are run with this last-named fuel.

The various experiments made to economize fuel for the "glory-holes," as the workmen call the working places above the furnace, are well known. For many years the prepared wood we have spoken of was used. Then resin in **a powdered** state was added, which was both inconvenient and dangerous, — it having caused the destruction by burning of two glass-houses. This risk was finally overcome by the introduction of an invention which used it in a liquid state. But **the** demand for resin **became so** great **as** soon to more than double its price. **This** led to the substitution of coal tar, which was in use until **science** discovered its latent virtues for other purposes, **and** largely increased the original **cost of** the material. Indeed, at first the gas companies had considered it of **no value, and had thrown** it away by thousands **of barrels.** Combined with dead oil it **is** still **used** by glass-makers, **but at** greatly enhanced prices.

The Cape Cod Glass Company have had in use for several years a Delano patent furnace-feeder, which **enables them to** use both hard and **soft** coal, **as either is** cheapest, and **consumes** the smoke and gas of either fuel, thus doing away all annoyance to the neighborhood. **Theretofore every** attempt to run working places **with** hard **or soft coal** had failed on account of the noxious gases **set free, which** injure the color of the glass. But owing to the **intense heat** created by the Delano patent, the furnace consumes these gases, and gives a quick fire polish to the various articles finished therein.

As our native supplies of hard and soft coal are inexhaustible, there **is no likelihood of an** increase in the price of the present fuel **so as to** necessitate, as heretofore, a substitution of some cheaper article, especially as the discovery of petroleum tends to cheapen **coal by a** diversion of a portion of **its consumption** to that useful **mineral oil.**

USEFUL ITEMS.

A bushel of English coal **weighs 80** pounds; of Virginia coal, **93** pounds; of Pictou, 76 pounds; of Cumberland, 84 pounds; of red ash, hard, 84 pounds.

Crude saltpetre, refined, loses nine per cent.

Chemists estimate that one hundred pounds of pearlash contain thirty per cent. carbonic acid. In refining, it loses on the average fifteen per cent. in weight.

Phosphate of soda brightens glass.

Borax brightens, but hardens glass.

Twenty-five silver dollars refined will give thirty-seven ounces of nitrate of silver.

A square foot of furnace clay weighs one hundred and twenty pounds.

Alum, calcined, loses in weight sixty per cent.

Crude flint batch, melted and ladled out, loses in the average fifteen per cent. in weight.

Hard coal will measure forty cubic feet to a gross ton.

Glass in water. There are some peculiar phenomena connected with hot glass and water. If a ball of red-hot iron is placed in a vessel containing cold water, the latter is quickly agitated. But a ball of melted glass of equal weight dropped in cold water will produce no immediate agitation. The water will remain for some time quiescent; but when the glass is cooled to about half its highest temperature, it agitates the cold water violently.

Technical terms, descriptive of glass, such as crystal, flint, tale, may be derived from these facts: the French used for their base crystal stones, burnt and ground fine; in England they had recourse only to flint stone, treated the same as the French used their blocks of crystal; tale was derived from the mode of selling, the best glass being sold only by weight, while light articles were sold tale.

www.ingramcontent.com/pod-product-compliance
Lightning Source LLC
Chambersburg PA
CBHW031354160426
43196CB00007B/805